Leading the Way: Major Japanese Corporations
[Second Edition]

日本を代表する企業で学ぶ

総合英語

〔改訂新版〕

小澤　健志 ● 小泉　和弘 ● 山崎　千秋
竹内　裕見子 ● 豊岡　めぐみ ● 早坂　裕介 ● 山下　理恵子

南雲堂

NAN'UN-DO

はしがき

本テキストは『日本を代表する企業で学ぶ総合英語』の改訂版であり、各企業のインターネット上の英語版 Web ページを本文としています[注)]。注釈が付けられた本文を読み、各種練習問題に解答していく構成になりますが、総合的な英語学習を行いながら企業研究も可能となるよう企画されたテキストです。

2008 年 9 月に起きたリーマンショック以来、世界の経済は低成長、低金利の時代に入りました。証券会社を中心に、金融機関や製造業などの多くの企業がリストラを断行し、長年続いた日本の終身雇用制も崩壊し、「大きな企業に入れば一生安泰」といった時代は遠く過ぎ去りました。

では、これから社会人になろうとする学生諸君はどうすれば良いのでしょうか。今までは就職と言っても「就社」でしたが、これからは文字どおり「就職」になると想定されます。過去において、企業は自分の組織内で色々な職種を経験させ、総合的な人材を育てようとしました。しかし、最近ではスペシャリストを求める傾向が見られ、営業職、経理職といった職種で募集する会社が増えています。このような現状を踏まえ、学生時代から専門性を磨くこと、そしてその専門性を育ててくれる会社を探すことが重要になります。このような観点から、どのような会社があり、その会社から何を学べるのかを知る上で、本テキストは有用であり、学生諸君のキャリアデザインの一助ともなるでしょう。その会社が将来どのようになろうとも、最初に入った会社で社会人としての基礎を学び、職の手ほどきを受けてスキルアップしていくことになるので、人材育成に重点を置いた会社を見つけることが望まれます。トヨタ自動車株式会社の社長でさえも「10 年後会社がどうなっているかは分からない」と述べており、本当に先のことは見通せませんが、各自の「職」のスキルアップを心がけ、努力してください。

最後になってしまいましたが、このようなテキストを作成する貴重な機会を与えてくださった南雲堂編集部の加藤敦課長、そして Web ページからの英文転載を快く承諾してくださった各企業に、心から感謝の意を表します。

2021 年 1 月

著者一同

Download Audio

音声ファイル
無料 DL
のご案内

このテキストの音声を無料で視聴（ストリーミング）・ダウンロードできます。自習用音声としてご活用ください。
以下のサイトにアクセスしてテキスト番号で検索してください。

https://nanun-do.com　テキスト番号［**512104**］

※ 無線 LAN（WiFi）に接続してのご利用を推奨いたします。

※ 音声ダウンロードは Zip ファイルでの提供になります。
お使いの機器によっては別途ソフトウェア（アプリケーション）の導入が必要となります。

Read by
Chris Koprowski
Emma Howard

※ Leading the Way [Second Edition] 音声ダウンロードページは以下の QR コードからもご利用になれます。

本書の構成

本書は 15 章で構成されていますが、各章とも、以下のパートから成り立っています。各パートには次のような目的がありますので、その趣旨を理解し、効率よく学習を進めてください。

Pre-Reading：Key Words　8 問

本文に出てくる重要な語の事前確認のための問題です。左側にある単語の各定義を、右側から選択してください。英英辞典の記述方法に慣れることが本問題の目的の一つですが、「英語を英語で理解するモード」に切り替えるつもりで、解答してみてください。

本文

各企業の英文ウェブページからの引用です。社長からのメッセージや企業理念や商品に関する説明文等が転載されています。商品によっては馴染みのない企業もあり、また企業理念等については未知なことも多く、難解に感じることがあるかもしれません。しかし、各社とも深く生活に密着している日本の企業であり、就職活動における「企業研究」のつもりで、よく読み込んでみてください。なお、速読を前提に、若干の語句説明を付してあります。

Exercise 1　5 問

本文の内容理解に関する問題です。英文を読み、その内容が本文と合っている場合には T を、間違っている、または述べられていない場合には F を答えてください。

Exercise 2　8 問

リスニングの問題です。重要な語や表現の聞き取りが特に問題になっていますが、年号や数字に関する聞き取りも含まれています。モードを切り替え、全神経を音声に集中するつもりで解答してください。

Exercise 3　3 問

リスニングと会話に関する練習問題です。まずはリスニングの問題になりますが、話題は企業の人等と交わす内容になります。空欄への補充が完了したら、基本的には二人組になり、当問題を会話練習として使ってください。「近いうちにこのような表現を使う」つもりで、コミュニケーション力アップのためにも、発話の練習をしてください。また、相手を代え、何回か練習し、表現の定着を図ってください。

Exercise 4　3 問

英作文のための問題です。「部品」は総て用意してありますので、これらを正しく組み立ててください。なお、このためには、文の組み立て方の規則である「文法」の知識が必要になります。文法について不安がある場合は、時間がかかったとしても、参考書等で確認してください。リスニングや会話においても、文法の知識は非常に重要です。

Exercise 5　2 問

前と同様に英作文の問題ですが、全文を作成することになります。冠詞の使い方から始まり、完璧な英作文を行うことは非常に難しいので、「正しい英文の組み立て方になっていて、趣旨が伝われば合格」と考え、頑張って英作文してみてください。ただし、ざっと英作文して終りではなく、時制等も含め、何回も確認と推敲を重ねてください。

注）各本文の Web ページ掲載時期は 2019 年秋になります。また、掲載内容を一部修正等した本文もあります。

CONTENTS

CHAPTER 1

味の素株式会社

Ajinomoto Co., Inc.

"Eat Well, Live Well."

Pre-Reading 1 : Key Words

❖ Match each word with its definition below.

＊The words are listed in the order in which they appear in the reading.

1. commercialize
2. aspiration
3. issue
4. launch
5. implement
6. adapt
7. wellness
8. infinite

(　　) a. to change something to make it suitable for a different purpose

(　　) b. without limits in space or time

(　　) c. an important topic or problem for debate or discussion

(　　) d. to make a product or service available for sale to the public

(　　) e. a strong desire to achieve something

(　　) f. to carry out; put into practice

(　　) g. to start; put into operation

(　　) h. the state of being in good health

Message to Investors

The Ajinomoto Group is a food company group whose growth has been driven by cutting-edge bioscience and [*1]fine chemical technologies with amino acids as our starting point. We are also the world's largest manufacturer of amino acids. The Ajinomoto story began in 1908, when [*2]Dr. Kikunae Ikeda, who wanted to "improve the [*3]nutrition of the Japanese people," discovered Umami and company founder [*4]Saburosuke Suzuki [Pre1]commercialized the discovery as the product Ajinomoto. Their [Pre2]aspiration of "Eat well, Live well."《「おいしく食べて健康づくり」》 has been carried on continuously in the form of Ajinomoto Group Creating Shared Value (ASV)《味の素グループ・シェアード・バリュー（ASV）》, an initiative《取り組み》 aimed at co-creating《共創する（こと）》 social value and economic value while helping resolve social [Pre3]issues. More than a century later, it remains the driving force behind the Group's every business development effort and the pursuit of globalization.

In April of 2017, we [Pre4]launched the [*5]FY2017-2019 (for 2020) Medium-Term Management Plan (the "Plan"). The new Management Plan provides a roadmap《指針》 for becoming a global top 10 class food company as a "Genuine Global《「確かなグローバル・》 Specialty Company."《スペシャリティ・カンパニー」》 The key objective《主要目標》 is to contribute to resolving issues facing human society in the 21st century by realizing our corporate slogan "Eat Well, Live Well." while vigorously [Pre5]implementing ASV [*6]group-wide across all of our businesses and in each region where we operate. To more steadily and surely accomplish this objective, we decided to newly set non-financial targets connected with our financial targets to be achieved through business activities and to formulate《策定する》 and share with our stakeholders ASV Integrated Targets《ASV総合目標》 combining financial and non-financial targets. The non-financial targets aim at contributing to the resolution of environmental and social issues and enhancing governance.

The environment for our business is expected to change rapidly, and changes may occur in international politics, various economic frameworks, and regulatory policy. I believe that it is precisely in such an environment that it is essential for us to share dialogue and initiatives with society, mainly with our shareholders and all other stakeholders, while continuing to move ahead with reforms to create a strong business structure capable of [Pre6]adapting to《～を進める》 circumstances. On that basis, we will aspire to achieve sustainable growth as a corporate group needed by society by steadily and surely achieving the ASV Integrated Targets beginning FY2017, the first year of the new Plan.

I request your continued support and encouragement.

What the Ajinomoto Group Aims for

3

To realize greater [Pre7]wellness for people all around the world through amino science—this is the Ajinomoto Group's promise to our customers.

Amino science is our unique scientific approach, enabling us to pursue the [Pre8]infinite possibilities of amino acids and provide products and services that support the health of the body and mind. We will continue to take on new challenges to make every day more comfortable and delicious《実に楽しい》.

出典 2019年秋の味の素株式会社Webページより転載

【Notes】

＊1 fine chemical: ファインケミカル。大量生産の工業薬品（heavy chemical）に対し、食品や医薬品などの分野で原料として利用される少量で高純度の精製化学製品、精薬品を指す。
＊2 Dr. Kikunae Ikeda: 池田菊苗博士（1864-1936）：戦前の化学者。
＊3 nutrition: 栄養状態
＊4 Saburosuke Suzuki: 鈴木三郎助（1868-1931）：実業家、味の素の創設者。
＊5 FY = fiscal year: 会計年度
＊6 group-wide: グループ全体で：副詞用法。

Exercise 1

❖ Read the sentences below. Write T if the sentence is true, F if it is false.

1. (　　) The Ajinomoto Group is enhancing its technological strength as the world's largest manufacturer of amino acids.

2. (　　) Amino acids are mainly used for animals needing medical treatment.

3. (　　) Umami was first identified by Dr. Kikunae Ikeda.

4. (　　) The Ajinomoto Group aims for the realization of a sustainable society to contribute to the world's food needs and nutritional well-being.

5. (　　) Amino science is a unique scientific approach mostly based on observation of and experimentation on human cells.

味の素株式会社

味の素グループは、先端バイオ・ファイン技術を核に、調味料、加工食品、飲料、アミノ酸、医薬品、化成品など幅広い分野で事業を展開するアミノ酸のリーディングカンパニーです。

1908年にアミノ酸の一種であるうま味成分のグルタミン酸を発見して以来、アミノ酸が持つ可能性を科学的に追求することで、世界中の人々の健やかな生活を支えてきました。同社はこれからも、“Eat Well, Live Well.”をコーポレートメッセージに、事業を通じて世界中の人々のウエルネスに貢献し、地域や社会とともに価値を創出することで、さらなる成長を目指しています。

味の素グループの2020年3月期の売上高は1兆1,000億円。世界35の国・地域に拠点を置き、商品を販売している国・地域は130以上にのぼります。

Exercise 2

❖ Listen to the sentences and fill in the blanks.

1. We can (   ) umami whenever it seems like (   ) is (   ) in our dishes.
2. Japanese cuisine offers a vast array of (   ) specialties (   ) with local (   ).
3. Glutamate (   ) naturally in the (   ) body and in many (   ) foods we eat every day.
4. Dr. Ikeda (   ) that the (   ) of umami was (   ) to glutamate.
5. "Umami" is (   ) from the four basic tastes of sweet, (   ), (   ) and salty.
6. (   ) speaking, the (   ) the amino acid level is, the (   ) the taste with umami is.
7. The (   ) amino acids are transported in the (   ) and distributed to (   ) throughout the body.
8. DNA plays a (   ) in (   ) amino acids to make (   ).

Exercise 3

❖ Listen and fill in the blanks in the short conversations below. Then practice the conversations with a partner.

1. *Student:* What are the (   ) of amino acids?

   Company: Amino acids offer many benefits. For example, they are (   ) nutrients for sports, helping the body improve (   ), (   ) recovery from fatigue and (   ) muscle soreness.

2. *Etsuko:* What's your (   ) of good health?

   Mutsuo: A proper diet and (   ) exercise are the keys to my healthy life. In (   ) to that, laughing and thinking (   ) are one way of (   ) with stress.

3. *Yutaka:* You seem to be a little (   ) the weather. Are you all right?

   Hajime: I was caught in a (   ), and I've been (   ) a little feverish since yesterday.

Exercise 4

❖ Rearrange the words and phrases to make correct sentences.

1. 味の素グループは、人々と地球の持続可能な未来の実現に取り組んでいる。
   The Ajinomoto Group (sustainable, future, achieve, working, people, earth, and, for, the, to, is, a).

2. 味の素 AFG は、コーヒー消費量の増加を受け、国内でのコーヒー栽培を計画している。
   Ajinomoto AFG plans (coffee trees, consumption, increases, Japan, grow, coffee, as, of, in, to).

3. アミノ酸は人間や地球上の他のすべての生物にとって不可欠です。
   Amino acids (essential, creature, humans, living, every, other, and, are, to) on the planet.

Exercise 5

❖ Translate into English.

1. 味の素グループ（the Ajinomoto Group）は、世界の食品会社トップ 10 に入ることを目指している。

2. アミノ酸（amino acids）は、クエン酸（citric acids）と並び、有名な有機化合物（organic compound）として挙げられている（be ranked with ～ as …）。

CHAPTER 2

花王株式会社

Kao Corporation

きれいを、こころに。未来に。

Pre-Reading 1 : Key Words

❖ Match each word with its definition below.

＊The words are listed in the order in which they appear in the reading.

1 . exceptional
2 . solid
3 . retail
4 . decline
5 . priority
6 . envision
7 . ethical
8 . attitude

(　　) a. the sale of goods to the public in relatively small quantities for use or consumption

(　　) b. much greater or better than usual

(　　) c. a settled way of thinking or feeling about something

(　　) d. to imagine as a future possibility

(　　) e. relating to moral principles

(　　) f. firm and stable

(　　) g. to become smaller, fewer or less

(　　) h. a thing that is regarded as more important than others

CEO Message

6

We aim to become a company with a global presence through our emphasis on profitable growth and [*1]ESG initiatives.

I would like to thank you, our [*2]shareholders, for your [Pre1]exceptional understanding and support of the Kao Group's business and corporate activities.

During the six months ended June 30, 2019, the markets for [*3]household and personal care products and cosmetics in Japan, which are key markets for the Kao Group, were in [Pre2]solid condition according to [Pre3]retail sales and consumer purchasing survey data. In every product category, the share of the e-commerce channel《Eコマースによる販売ルートの占有率》 increased further.

花王株式会社

Under these circumstances, the Cosmetics Business performed strongly, the baby diapers《赤ちゃん用オムツ》 are on a recovery track《回復軌道に乗って》, and with the impact of selling price adjustments associated with a [Pre4]decline in prices for natural fats and oils《天然油脂》 in the Chemical Business, net sales《純売上高》 decreased 1.0% compared with the same period a year earlier to 721.4 billion yen. [*4]On a like-for-like basis, net sales decreased 0.2%. Operating income was 86.4 billion yen, a decrease of 4.4 billion yen compared with the same period a year earlier. The interim dividend《中間配当金》 was 65 yen per share《1株につき》, an increase of 5 yen compared with the same period a year earlier. Despite the severe business environment, we will continue our efforts to achieve our forecast of consolidated operating results《連結業績》.

By 2030, the Kao Group intends to make Kao a company with a global presence and take it to the next level by achieving its goals: (1) a distinctive《特長のある》 corporate image, (2) a high-profit global consumer goods company that exceeds 2.5 trillion yen in net sales (1.0 trillion yen outside Japan), a 17% operating《営業》 margin《利益率》 and 20% [*5]ROE, and (3) a high level of returns to [*6]stakeholders.

As social conditions and the natural environment are changing dramatically, the Kao Group considers not only financial strategies but also non-financial strategies and initiatives《取り組み》 to be one of its top management [Pre5]priorities, and developed and launched the "Kirei* Lifestyle Plan" in April 2019 as its ESG strategy, which realizes lifestyles that people desire. To help create the future that people worldwide [Pre6]envision, we will take an approach unique to the

Kao Group in squarely《真摯に、公明正大に》 confronting social issues raised by [*7]the Sustainable Development Goals (SDGs) and addressing matters, such as the strengthening of environmental laws and regulations and the [Pre7]ethical actions of consumers. The Kao Group will thoroughly instill《浸透させる》 the [*8]“Integrity” set forth《記述する、規定する》 in the Kao Way, the Group’s corporate philosophy《企業理念》, by sharing and practicing it among all employees, while promoting both profitable growth and contributions to the sustainability of society.

I would appreciate your continued understanding and support of the Kao Group’s business and corporate activities.

* The Japanese word “Kirei” describes something that is clean, well-ordered and beautiful, all at the same time. For Kao, this concept of Kirei not only describes appearance《外見》, but also [Pre8] [*9]attitude—to seek to create beauty for oneself, and also for other people and for the natural world around us.

August 2019

出典 https://www.kao.com/global/en/investor-relations/management-information/top-message/

【Notes】

＊1 ESG: Environment（環境）、Social（社会）、Governance（ガバナンス）の頭文字で、企業の価値を測る基準とされる。
＊2 shareholder: 株主。stockholder と同義語である。
＊3 household and personal care products: 洗剤やトイレタリー、スキンケアなどのコンシューマー向け用品。
＊4 On a like-for-like basis: 既存店ベースで。今年度の売上を、新規店舗などを含まず前年度と同じ条件で比較すること。
＊5 ROE: return on equity（自己資本利益率）の略。自己資本（純資産）に対してどれだけの利益が生み出されたのかを示す財務分析の指標。
＊6 stakeholder: ステークホルダー。会社の業績で利害関係が生じる人を指す。なお、ステークホルダーは株主であるとは限らない。
＊7 the Sustainable Development Goals (SDGs): 持続可能な開発目標。持続可能な世界を実現するために 2015 年 9 月の国連サミットで採択された 2016 年から 2030 年までの国際目標。
＊8 “Integrity”: 企業理念である「花王ウェイ」においては、「正道を歩む」（法と倫理に則って行動し、誠実で清廉な事業活動を行なうこと、企業にとっての「信用」や「けじめ」を含む）という意味で用いられている。なお、integrity は多義性の強い語であり、a lack of integrity は「道徳心［けじめ］のなさ」、the integrity of an organization なら「組織の信頼性［健全性］」という解釈が可能であり、次例の大リーグ球団 the Houston Astros のサイン盗みを報じた記事に登場する integrity は「公正性」のような意味で使われている。Manfred acknowledged that baseball’s perceived “integrity” problem has inflicted “significant harm to the game.” — *TIME*, Jan. 27, 2020
＊9 attitude: 感じ方・考え方、心の在り方

Exercise 1

❖ Read the sentences below. Write T if the sentence is true, F if it is false.

1. (　　) More Kao products have been sold online recently.

2. (　　) The sales of all Kao products showed a drastic increase in 2019.

3. (　　) There were price hikes in some materials in chemical products.

4. (　　) The dividend per share received by a shareholder in 2019 was 70 yen.

5. (　　) Kao will contribute to tackling social problems.

花王株式会社

1887 年創業の老舗であり、戦前には桐の箱に入った花王石鹸は高級な贈答品として知られていました。現在では「きれいを、こころに。未来に。」をメッセージとして、事業の持続的な成長と社会の持続性を目指して活動しています。

花王石鹸ホワイト、入浴剤バブ、食器用洗剤キュキュット、洗濯用洗剤アタックなど身近で良く知られた商品を多く製造しています。トイレタリーは国内首位で、化粧品も大手です。原料からの一貫生産をしており、独自の物流、販売網も所有しています。

会社として「花王ウェイ」を全ての活動の根幹にすえ、世界の人々の喜びと満足のある豊かな生活文化を実現すると共に、社会のサステナビリティ（持続可能性）に貢献することを使命としています。2030 年までに低環境負荷の高機能品 10 以上の投入、製品の小型化による大量輸送、太陽光設備促進等で二酸化炭素排出量を 22%減（2017 年比）を目標としています。

Exercise 2

❖ Listen to the sentences and fill in the blanks.

1. Kao has (　　　　　　　) to (　　　　　　　) its contribution to society through a (　　　　　　　) focus on ESG.
2. The ESG (　　　　　　　) is in service to our consumers' needs, (　　　　　　　) and desires to live (　　　　　　　) lifestyles.
3. The company is stepping up (　　　　　　　) to support its (　　　　　　　) in living a beautiful life, (　　　　　　　) and out.
4. The "Kao Way" (　　　　　　　) our corporate philosophy and is the (　　　　　　　) of the business (　　　　　　　) of the Kao Group.
5. The "Kao Way" provides (　　　　　　　) to Group activities, from the (　　　　　　　) of mid- to long-term business plans to each business (　　　　　　　) that the firm makes every day.
6. The "Kao Way" acts as a guiding (　　　　　　　) for all corporate members, bringing together the (　　　　　　　) of the company and that of its (　　　　　　　) members.
7. Changes cannot (　　　　　　　) in society if no one (　　　　　　　) leading (　　　　　　　).
8. Kao products and (　　　　　　　) of (　　　　　　　) value are created from the consumer's and customer's (　　　　　　　).

Exercise 3

❖ Listen and fill in the blanks in the short conversations below. Then practice the conversations with a partner.

1. *Student:* What was the first product sold by Kao?
   Company: It was *Kao Sekken*, or *Kao Soap*, which was (　　　　　　　) in 1890. It was an (　　　　　　　) but high-quality (　　　　　　　) soap made in Japan.

2. *Student:* Is your company selling other (　　　　　　　) of products now?
   Company: Yes. For example, Kao holds a top share of the market for (　　　　　　　) detergents. Kao Group is also (　　　　　　　) the cosmetics market.

3. *Student:* Does Kao also sell their products (　　　　　　　)?
   Company: Of course. The company is (　　　　　　　) around the globe. (　　　　　　　) in Asia is particularly high.

Exercise 4

❖ Rearrange the words and phrases to make correct sentences.

1. 花王の使命の１つは、社会のサステナビリティに貢献することです。
   One of Kao's missions (sustainability, contribute, society, the, to, of, to, is).

2. 花王は自社の製品容器に用いられるプラスチックの量を減らすことに尽力している。
   Kao (committed, reducing, amount, plastic, used, the, of, in, to, is) its product containers.

3. 「メリーズ」は、肌に優しい赤ちゃん用おむつの高級ブランドです。
   "Merries" is a premium brand (gentle, diapers, that, baby, skin, are, the, of, on).

Exercise 5

❖ Translate into English.

1. 私たちは常に消費者を第一に考えています（give first priority to）。

2. 工場に設置された（installed in）ソーラーパネルは、二酸化炭素排出（CO_2 emissions）の削減につながる。

CHAPTER 3

CYBERDYNE 株式会社

CYBERDYNE Inc.

装着型サイボーグで新産業創成に挑戦する
ベンチャー企業

Pre-Reading 1 : Key Words

❖ Match each word with its definition below.

＊The words are listed in the order in which they appear in the reading.

1．valuable
2．field
3．found
4．define
5．philosophy
6．realize
7．treat
8．approve

(　　) a. to describe exactly
(　　) b. to give medical care to
(　　) c. to establish; start (an organization, company, etc.)
(　　) d. important
(　　) e. to officially accept; permit
(　　) f. an area of activity, study, etc.
(　　) g. to achieve something that you have planned or hoped for
(　　) h. a theory or attitude that acts as a guiding principle for behavior

MESSAGE

"Dreams" and "Passion" are [Pre1]valuable, but "Empathy" is much more important. If one has empathy for people and society, one cannot stand idly by《ただ傍観する》, but will proactively《積極的に》 think and take immediate actions for a brighter future. This is the heart of CYBERDYNE.

出典 https://www.cyberdyne.jp/english/company/index.html

CYBERDYNE Inc. develops products and services based on [*1]Cybernics Technologies in the [Pre2]fields of medicine, nursing care, workplaces and daily life. As a venture company developed to solve various social problems facing the super-aged society, CYBERDYNE Inc. was [Pre3]founded in June 2004 by [*2]Yoshiyuki Sankai, a professor at the University of Tsukuba in Ibaraki Prefecture, Japan, who established Cybernics, an academic field that is [Pre4]defined as the fusion of humans, robots and information systems. Under the [Pre5]philosophy that technology exists for humans and society, the company promotes social innovation with innovative Cybernics Systems. One of its novel products is the world's first Wearable Cyborg HAL® (Hybrid Assistive Limb), which [Pre6]realizes the wearer's intended motion via《～を介して》 neurological signals commanding the movements.

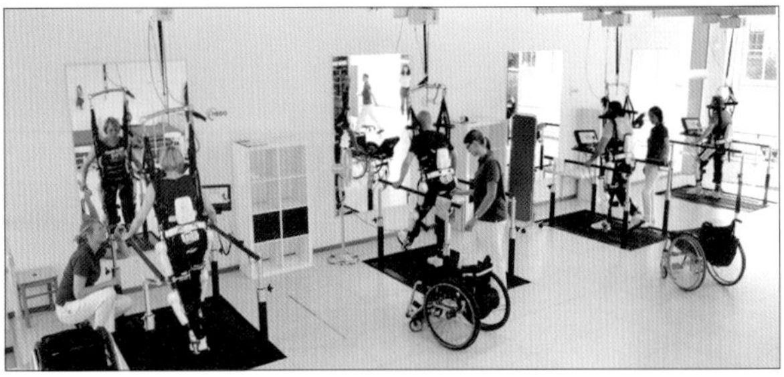

出典 https://www.cyberdyne.jp/english/company/index.html

HAL® can be used in many ways, such as for [Pre7]treating physically challenged persons《障がい者》. Even for people with disabilities, HAL® can detect their intent to move through the sensors attached on the surface of the skin. This helps the wearer carry out the intended motion. When the movement is realized, sensory information《感覚情報》 is fed back to the brain. HAL® helps the wearer formulate《構築する》 this [*3]neurological loop, which induces《もたらす》 the improvement of the《脳・》 brain-nerve-musculoskeletal-systems《神経・筋骨格系》. HAL® is now being used in hospitals of different countries, treating patients who have difficulty moving their bodies.

出典 https://www.cyberdyne.jp/english/products/HAL/index.html
ttps://www.cyberdyne.jp/company/download/20191001_AnnualReport_en.pdf Cybernics Treatment

12

Innovation drove the development of new areas around the world, and although this didn't happen overnight, it still led to major industrial and social changes. First it was the robot industry. Then it was the IT industry. Our company will be the next challenger to bring about the new wave of innovation. HAL® for Medical Use, which was [Pre8]approved as a medical device in Japan, the United States and Europe, is now being offered to hospitals in Asia and the Middle East as well. In this way, we are accelerating our efforts to formulate a platform that will be used on a global scale.

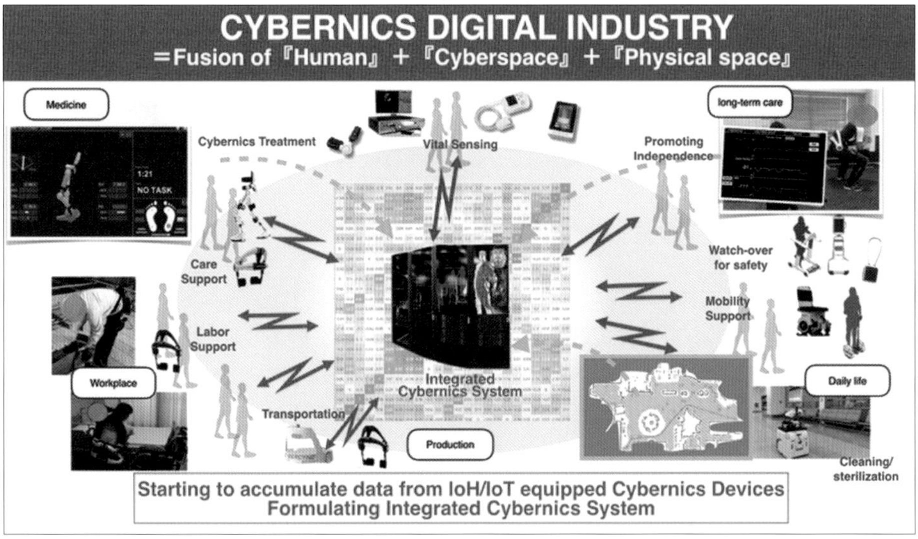

出典 https://www.cyberdyne.jp/company/download/20191001_AnnualReport_en.pdf
To our stakeholders 第3段落

【Notes】

＊1 Cybernics Technologies: サイバニクス技術。人・ロボット・情報系の融合複合技術。
＊2 Yoshiyuki Sankai: 山海嘉之 (1958-)。筑波大学システム情報系教授。サイバニクス学者、ロボット工学者。CYBERDYNE の創業者兼 CEO。筑波大学サイバニクス研究センター研究統括 (2017.10 ～)。2019 年 11 月 3 日紫綬褒章受章。
＊3 neurological loop: 神経系ループ。「ループ」は「連鎖」の意。

Exercise 1

❖ Read the sentences below. Write T if the sentence is true, F if it is false.

1. (　　) The world's first Wearable Cyborg HAL® is made for the purpose of improving and regenerating patients' physical function.

2. (　　) HAL® can detect faint bio-electrical signals from the brain and nerve systems.

3. (　　) Cyberdyne believes that technology only makes sense if it benefits people and society.

4. (　　) The practical use of HAL® has raised expectations in the field of the military industry for years.

5. (　　) When a patient wears HAL®, it becomes possible to estimate the progression of their disease and the extent of the damage caused.

CYBERDYNE 株式会社

筑波大学発のベンチャー企業です。2014年に東証マザーズ市場に上場しました。医療・福祉をはじめとする幅広い業界に対して、製品のレンタルを行っており、海外売り上げ17%です。

主力商品は、世界初の装着型サイボーグHAL®で、身体機能を改善・補助・再生することができ、既に欧州・アメリカ・日本・東南アジアの複数国でも医療機器認証を取得しています。人が体を動かそうとすると、その運動意思に従って脳から神経を通じて筋肉に信号が伝わり、その際、微弱な「生体電位信号」が体表に漏れ出して来ます。その信号を装着者の皮膚に貼ったセンサーで検出し、意思に従った動作を実現します。同時に、動作が実現されると身体内部の感覚神経系の情報が脳へフィードバックされると考えられており、この独特なループによって機能改善・機能再生を促します。医療用ばかりではなく、介護支援用・作業支援用もあり、介護者や作業者が腰を痛めるリスクを減らしています。

高齢化がますます進む社会において、介護の需要もますます増加することが見込まれ、装着型ロボットの需要も広がると思われています。

Exercise 2

❖ Listen to the sentences and fill in the blanks. 13

1. Cyberdyne, founded on June 24, 2004, is a (   ) company to (   ) and distribute the (   ) Cyborg HAL®.
2. HAL® can support workers with physically (   ) jobs, reducing the (   ) of injury of users.
3. Technology that can (   ) read a massive (   ) of data will have an important (   ) to play in medical research.
4. Human (   ) is a complex interplay of three (   ): reason, will and (   ).
5. HAL® has (   ) beyond the medical field, with everything from (   ) work to elderly (   ).
6. Wearable Cyborg HAL®s use brain-derived (   ) to (   ) people's ability to (   ).
7. When a person moves their body, various (   ) are sent from the brain to their (   ) through (   ).
8. Japan's lead in advanced (   ) for healthcare is (   ) by demographic (   ).

Exercise 3

❖ Listen and fill in the blanks in the short conversations below. Then practice the conversations with a partner. 14

1. *Student:* I wonder what the (   ) of your company name is.

   Company: Cyberdyne is the (   ) of "cybernics" and the suffix "-dyne" referring to (   ). Our name is not (   ) to the Cyberdyne Systems that produced villainous (   ) in the US sci-fi Terminator film. We create robots for peace and (   ).

2. *Shizuko:* Do you think robots will (   ) humans in the workplace (   )?

   Kazuhiko: I don't think so, but artificial intelligence (   ) the automation of (   ) work.

3. *Hitomi:* What is the difference (   ) humans and robots?

   Shuhei: The point is (   ) it is possible to deal (   ) every situation (   ).

Exercise 4

❖ Rearrange the words and phrases to make correct sentences.

1. 皮膚に取り付けられた小さなセンサーが、装着者の体の微弱な生体電気信号を検出する。
   Small sensors (bio-electrical, signals, faint, placed, detect, skin, the, on) in a wearer's body.

   ____

   ____

2. 装着型デバイスは、工場労働者の生産性を向上することにも役立っている。
   Wearable devices (productivity, workers, helping, factory, boost, also, are).

   ____

   ____

3. サイバニクス治療は機能的再生治療として世界中のマスコミから注目されている。
   Cybernics Treatment (international, attention, attracted, media, has, as) a functional regenerative treatment.

   ____

   ____

Exercise 5

❖ Translate into English.

1. その装置は、装着者（wearer）が必要な力を発揮（exert）できるようにする。

   ____

   ____

2. HAL® は、介護者が患者を持ち上げるのを支援する強力なツールです。

   ____

   ____

CHAPTER 4

サントリーホールディングス株式会社

Suntory Holdings Limited

水と生きる

Pre-Reading 1 : Key Words

❖ Match each word with its definition below.

＊The words are listed in the order in which they appear in the reading.

1. insistence
2. thorough
3. commitment
4. synergy
5. priority
6. conserve
7. will
8. foster

(　　) a. complete; absolute

(　　) b. the combined power of two or more things when they are working together

(　　) c. something that is very important and must be done first

(　　) d. a very firm statement that something is true or should be done

(　　) e. to help something to develop over a period of time

(　　) f. to protect something from damage, harm or destruction

(　　) g. a promise or firm decision to do something

(　　) h. the mental power used to control and direct your thoughts or actions

Helping Suntory be a "Growing for Good" Global Company

The Suntory Group continues to enjoy steady growth in a wide range of global businesses centered around the sales of alcoholic beverages and soft drinks. Through our corporate philosophy, "To create harmony with people and nature," we have since our founding《創業》 contributed to the richness of people's lives by providing the highest quality products and services to our customers, and have aimed to《～することを目指す》 realize a sustainable society through harmony with nature—always coexisting《共存する》 with the beautiful, global environment. To promote these efforts on a global scale, this year we established the [*1]"Suntory Group Sustainability Vision." With this policy as our guiding principle《指針》, we will continue to promote sustainable management on a global level, and work toward becoming a company that is [*2]"Growing for Good."

Even as《ちょうど～である時も》 our business expands across the globe, our [Pre1]insistence on quality remains unchanged. With customer satisfaction first, and safety a must《必須なもの》, we maintain our [Pre2]thorough [Pre3]commitment to product quality in the customer experience《顧客体験》, from the taste of our products to the ease《容易さ》 of use of our product containers. As a global company, Suntory Group continues to create new value for our audiences《顧客（層）》 by developing high-quality products through finding [Pre4]synergies across national and corporate boundaries. In recent years, Suntory has created many innovative products by combining its 120-year heritage of craftsmanship《職人技》 with the strength of our overseas group companies that own《所有する》 many locally loved brands. We will continue to promote activities that deliver new value to our customers' lifestyles around the world through using our strengths as a global company to the greatest extent《最大限に》.

Based on our founding spirit of [*3]"Giving Back to Society," we consider it to be our great mission to hand down《～を後世に伝える》 a sustainable society with a rich natural environment to the next generation through our unique efforts. The greatest [Pre5]priority across our efforts《私たちの取り組み全体で》 is supporting the sustainability of water, which is the source of our business as well as a precious resource supporting human life. As a company that places water as its core, we have been engaged for many years in a variety of efforts to [Pre6]conserve and educate about this important resource in Japan. Now, using the knowledge we developed in Japan, we are rolling out《本格的に展開する》 our water sustainability efforts globally. In Europe and the United States, we have partnered with local organizations to promote environmental preservation activities including those aimed at developing sustainable water resources. In Southeast Asia, we conduct water education programs for children to teach about the importance of water and nature to the next generation and leaders of the future. We will continue to expand and carry out our efforts around water, in line with《～に沿って》 local needs, in all regions where we conduct business.

It is the strength of our Suntory Group employees that turns our [Pre7]will into reality. The driving force《原動力》 behind our activities is the spirit of [＊4]"Yatte Minahare," passed down since our founding. By [Pre8]fostering an environment where all our employees can put the spirit of "Yatte Minahare" into practice《実践》, we will continue to take on unique challenges to innovate and build a brighter society.

出典 https://www.suntory.com/about/topmessage (2019 年 8 月時点)

SUNTORY

【Notes】

＊1 "Suntory Group Sustainability Vision": 「サントリーグループ　サステナビリティ・ビジョン」。2019 年に策定された、持続可能な社会を実現するための重要課題・行動目標。

＊2 "Growing for Good": 「世の中に良いことを提供するためにこそ成長する」。より良い社会と環境の実現を図りながら、自社が成長すること。

＊3 "Giving Back to Society": 「利益三分主義」。利益を「事業への再投資」だけでなく、'おかげさまで' の心で「得意先・取引先へのサービス」や「社会への貢献」にも役立てること。

＊4 "Yatte Minahare": 「やってみなはれ」は、誰もやらなかったことに挑み、失敗や反対を恐れず挑戦し続けるチャレンジ精神。創業以来、原動力となってきた価値観。

Exercise 1

❖ Read the sentences below. Write T if the sentence is true, F if it is false.

1. (　　) The Suntory Group has been growing globally in the main business of selling alcoholic beverages and soft drinks.

2. (　　) Suntory has recently created various innovative products without relying on its craftsmanship.

3. (　　) Suntory believes that supporting the sustainability of water is a very important mission for human beings.

4. (　　) Suntory's water education programs for children in Southeast Asia have little effect on teaching about the importance of water and nature.

5. (　　) The Suntory Group is driven by"Yatte Minahare"—the spirit of bold ambition.

サントリーホールディングス株式会社

創業者である鳥井信治郎が、1899 年に大阪市に「鳥井商店」を開業し、葡萄酒の製造販売を始めたのが元となる会社です。鳥井は「日本人の味覚に合った洋酒をつくり、日本の洋酒文化を切り拓きたい」という理想を持ち、1921 年に「株式会社寿屋」を創立しました。

1907 年には「赤玉ポートワイン」を発売し、斬新なネーミング、ボトルデザイン、宣伝広告も相まって大ヒットしました。「やってみなはれ」精神で、山崎の地に日本初のウイスキー蒸留所を誕生させ、1923 年に本格的ウイスキー作りに乗り出しました。1963 年に「サントリービール」を発売し、同年「寿屋」から「サントリー株式会社」に社名を変更しました。2013 年には、連結決算子会社として「サントリー食品インターナショナル」を東証 1 部に上場させ、2019 年 12 月期の売上高は 2 兆 5,692 億円（酒税込み）に達しました。

Exercise 2

❖ Listen to the sentences and fill in the blanks. 16

1. Founded as a family-(　　　　) business in 1899 in Osaka, the Suntory Group has grown into a multi-(　　　　) corporation.
2. Because it takes years to (　　　　) unblended whisky, Suntory is constructing a number of (　　　　) facilities.
3. Since our founding, we have consistently created new (　　　　) by harnessing the (　　　　) of technology and the expertise of our (　　　　).
4. We will (　　　　) to be a company where all employees take up the (　　　　) to create new (　　　　), moving freely like water.
5. We have developed (　　　　) products such as *Sesamin* brands (　　　　) the health ingredient sesamin.
6. With the (　　　　) of Suntory Museum of Art and Suntory Hall, the company has increased its contribution to (　　　　) life.
7. Suntory believes that businesses should (　　　　) their profits with (　　　　).
8. Suntory succeeded in developing the world's (　　　　) blue rose in 2004. It had been considered (　　　　) to create.

Exercise 3

❖ Listen and fill in the blanks in the short conversations below. Then practice the conversations with a partner. 17

1. *Yutaka:* What do you (　　　　) of the company (　　　　) of Suntory?
   Naoko: Well, its (　　　　) and color (　　　　) me of fresh (　　　　).

2. *Student:* Is it safe to drink very old (　　　　)?
   Company: As long as it is (　　　　) and in a good state of (　　　　), you can drink it because whisky is distilled and high-proof (　　　　).

3. *Mao:* I hear you're a beer person. What (　　　　) of beer do you like best?
   Chihiro: I would say there is (　　　　) (　　　　) Suntory's Premium Malt's.

Exercise 4

❖ Rearrange the words and phrases to make correct sentences.

1. その企業グループは、水を育む森を守り、社会の必要を満たしています。
   The company group (satisfies, cultivate, forests, protects, water, that, and, the) the needs of society.

2. 自然環境を次世代に引き継ぐことは非常に重要です。
   It is very important (environment, generation, natural, pass, next, on, the, the, to, to).

3. その会社はまた、価値のあるサービスを社会に提供することで、私たちの生活を豊かにしています。
   They also (delivering, services, enrich, society, value, lives, our, to, of, by).

Exercise 5

❖ Translate into English.

1. 世界中の何百万人もの人々が、その会社が製造する様々な種類の飲料 (beverage) を愛飲しています (enjoy)。

2. 水は最も重要な経営資源 (management resource) であるだけでなく、万人に共有される貴重な資源 (a vital resource) でもあります。

CHAPTER 5

Spiber株式会社

Spiber Inc.

次世代基幹産業を目指すベンチャー企業

Pre-Reading 1 : Key Words

❖ Match each word with its definition below.

＊The words are listed in the order in which they appear in the reading.

1. master
2. sustainable
3. feedstock
4. issue
5. via
6. pioneer
7. address
8. sophisticated

(　　) a. a problem that needs to be considered
(　　) b. to deal with; tackle; combat
(　　) c. by means of
(　　) d. raw material that is used in an industrial process
(　　) e. to make full use of something
(　　) f. able to last or continue for a long time
(　　) g. highly developed and complex
(　　) h. to be the first to do or use something

Mastering Proteins as a Solution

Metal. Glass. Petrochemicals. Humanity has [Pre1]mastered a wide variety of raw materials and achieved enormous progress throughout its brief history. Now, proteins are poised《ready; set》 to become a [Pre2]sustainable next-generation material with potential [*1]unlike any the world has ever seen. [*2]It all starts with spider silk, which is 340 times tougher than steel. Protein materials《タンパク質素材》 are environmentally friendly, highly customizable, and have incredible functionality. They have the capacity to expand into an entire platform for《～の基盤》 material development; a multitude of different proteins can be produced using the same [Pre3]feedstock and processes. For the last eleven years we have been using spider silk as a stepping-stone, making steady progress toward not simply《not just [only]》 understanding proteins, but mastering them.

「ブリュード・プロテイン™と各種加工工程で得られた素材の例」

出典 Spiber's homepage 2018

Cost Barrier

Presently, synthetic《人工的な》 protein materials do not enjoy widespread adoption《広範に普及する》 due largely to the [Pre4]issue of cost. As an example, it is often said within the fermentation industry that producing genetically modified proteins《遺伝子組み換えタンパク質》 [Pre5]via microbial fermentation《微生物発酵》 for less than $100 per kilogram is extremely difficult. Spiber calls this phenomenon the 'Hundred Dollar Barrier.' [*3]To put this figure into context, analysis of the global polymer《ポリマー、重合体》 market suggests that the threshold《境界値》 for widespread adoption of a material is approximately $20-30 per kilogram. Gaining access to《～への参入》 larger markets—those in excess of《～を上回る》 ten billion dollars—requires lowering the cost to less than $10 per kilogram. The gap between the cost of proteins produced via fermentation and the cost necessary to attain widespread adoption is vast, and [Pre6]pioneering a new market requires massive investment. These factors are responsible for《～の原因となっている》 the dearth《lack》 of synthetic protein materials on the market today.

出典 Spiber's homepage 2018

Innovative Solutions

20

Overcoming the high cost of synthetic protein materials was considered by some《some people》 to be a nearly impossible task. Spiber has worked since 2007 to solve this problem, developing cutting edge《最先端の》 technologies and pursuing increased efficiency《効率性の向上》 in the protein design《タンパク質設計》 and production process.

「構造タンパク質を使った世界初のアウトドアジャケット「MOON PARKA®」(日本限定 50 着 / 2019 年 12 月発売。価格￥150,000 (税抜)) 株式会社ゴールドウインとの共同研究開発による商品。MOON PARKA は Spiber 株式会社と株式会社ゴールドウインの商標です。」

When Spiber was first established, there was no single team in the world that possessed all of the necessary technology and know-how to [Pre7]address the considerable challenge《大きな難関》 of producing synthetic protein materials at commercial scale《商業規模で》. Undaunted, Spiber set about《着手した》 designing《考案(すること)》 novel solutions from scratch《ゼロから》. These included technologies for designing proteins, gene synthesis and recombination《遺伝子の合成と組み換え》, fermentation and purification《精製》, and spinning and processing《紡糸加工》. While developing these core technologies in-house, Spiber worked to break down barriers of specialization《専門(分野)》 and built a research environment conducive to《～への道が開ける》 interdisciplinary《学際的な》 thinking. Even now, there still exist a daily myriad of problems spanning《～にまたがる》 multiple technological domains《技術領域》, but efforts must continue to develop ever more [Pre8]sophisticated and streamlined《合理化された》 approaches in order to achieve lower costs. The result of all this hard work has been enormous: compared to when Spiber started in 2007, productivity and cost have dramatically improved, bringing Spiber's materials to a place where large scale adoption is finally becoming a reality.

出典 Spiber's homepage 2018

【Notes】

＊1 unlike any the world has ever seen: 世界がこれまで(素材として)注目したことがない e.g. This particular U.S. election is *unlike any other* we have lived through. (Direct Mail from *The Washington Post*, Nov. 3, 2020)

＊2 It all starts with: タンパク質を基幹素材の候補と考えた契機は～である

＊3 To put this figure into context: このコスト金額を実状に照らしてみると

Exercise 1

❖ Read the sentences below. Write T if the sentence is true, F if it is false.

1. (　　) Natural spider silk is seen as the only key to mastering protein materials.

2. (　　) The venture business Spiber now stands at the dawn of the era of practical application of synthetic protein materials.

3. (　　) Synthetic protein materials are expected to come into widespread use when their production costs are reduced.

4. (　　) The process of producing a synthetic protein includes genetic modification.

5. (　　) Few researchers at Spiber hope to mass-produce the synthetic protein on an industrial scale.

Spiber 株式会社

サステナブルな新素材を開発するバイオベンチャー。独自開発する構造タンパク質「ブリュード・プロテイン」は、ブリューイング（微生物による発酵）によりつくられ、原料を石油や動物に依存しないため、アパレル分野や輸送機器、毛髪、建築材料、医療分野等における脱プラスチック・脱アニマルのニーズに対し、大きな役割を果たす可能性を秘めている。2007 年の設立以来、総額 300 億円以上の資金を調達（2019 年時点）し、サステナブルな社会の実現のためにタンパク質素材の開発を進める。現在タイに世界最大規模のブリュード・プロテイン生産拠点を建設中。

Exercise 2

❖ Listen to the sentences and fill in the blanks. 21

1. A ( ) or obvious question is often what leads to a ( ) that drives significant ( ).
2. Humanity faces a ( ) of ( ) issues that must be ( ).
3. Synthetic ( ) materials that are not made from oil could become a ( )-generation ( ) material.
4. We ( ) proteins as a ( ) new ( ) of materials.
5. Every person ( ) to society in some ( ), and we all reap the ( ) of these contributions.
6. We aspire to ( ) grave environmental destruction, the crisis of ( ) resources, war and ( ) crimes.
7. Spiber's ( ) statement is "( ) global problems through the power of protein-( ) materials."
8. The name "Brewed Protein™" is ( ) with Spiber's proprietary ( ), or brewing, ( ).

Exercise 3

❖ Listen and fill in the blanks in the short conversations below. Then practice the conversations with a partner. 22

1. *Student:* What is the ( ) and meaning of Spiber?
   Company: Our name "Spiber" is a ( ) of the two words "spider" and "( )."

2. *Student:* When and where was your ( ) established?
   Company: Our venture firm was ( ) on September 26, ( ), and the head office is ( ) in Tsuruoka City, Yamagata Prefecture.

3. *Shizuko:* ( ) do you think is the moral of Ryunosuke Akutagawa's ( ) story *The Spider's* ( )?
   Kazuhiko: I would ( ) the lesson is that we can be egoistic and self-( ).

Exercise 4

❖ Rearrange the words and phrases to make correct sentences.

1. タンパク質素材は持続可能な工業用基幹材料となる可能性を秘めている。
   Protein materials (mainstay industrial materials, serve, potential, sustainable, have, the, to, as).

2. 「ブリュード・プロテイン」と呼ばれる夢の繊維は、石油由来ではないゆえ、画期的な新素材として注目されるようになった。
   The dream fiber called "Brewed Protein" (a groundbreaking material, because, attracted, attention, has, are, its raw materials, as) not derived from petroleum.

3. スパイバーは原料に石油などの枯渇資源に頼らない構造タンパク質を独自技術で生成している。
   Spiber has proprietary technologies (without, produce, using, resources, structural proteins, exhaustible, to) such as oil as their raw materials.

Exercise 5

❖ Translate into English.

1. その会社は、業界の専門家と連携して（in cooperation with)、研究開発や事業開発を加速させています。

2. 近い将来、タンパク質は基幹素材 (a basic industrial material) として広く使われるだろう。

CHAPTER 6

セコム株式会社

SECOM CO., LTD.

あらゆる不安のない社会をつくる

Pre-Reading 1 : Key Words

❖ Match each word with its definition below.

＊The words are listed in the order in which they appear in the reading.

1 . reliable
2 . declare
3 . collaboration
4 . diverse
5 . foundation
6 . domestic
7 . overseas
8 . enhancement

(　　) a. the action of working with someone to produce something
(　　) b. relating to a foreign country
(　　) c. an underlaying basis or principle
(　　) d. to announce something officially
(　　) e. existing inside a particular country, not foreign
(　　) f. an increase or improvement in quality, value, or extent
(　　) g. able to be trusted
(　　) h. showing a great deal of variety

A Message from the President

23

Established in 1962, SECOM is recognized as Japan's first security services《警備保障》 provider《会社》. Since then, we have been providing [Pre1]reliable peace of mind with our strong desire to create services that benefit society, in line with《〜に沿って》 our social《社会的》 mission《使命》 of helping to achieve a society free from concerns.

SECOM has sought to develop innovative services, launching Japan's first on-line commercial security system in 1966, and home security system in 1981.

In 1989, SECOM [Pre2]declared its commitment to creating the Social System Industry《社会システム産業》, which is a framework《枠組み》 that delivers safety, peace of mind, comfort and convenience that are essential in daily life. Today, our business portfolio《事業ポートフォリオ》 encompasses《包括する》 security services, fire protection services, medical services, insurance services, geospatial information services《地理空間情報サービス》, [*1]BPO and [*2]ICT services, and real estate《不動産》 and other services. We also actively expand outside Japan, currently providing security services in 13 countries and territories, and establishing presences in a total of 18 countries and territories as the SECOM Group.

警備員がお客様のもとに駆けつけて対応

Operating in an environment characterized by drastic change and mounting uncertainty《増大する不確実性》, with the aim to further speed the realization of the Social System Industry, in 2017, we formulated《策定する》 the SECOM Group's Vision for 2030, which positions 2030 as a [*3]milestone. As part of our vision, we are working to create [*4]the ANSHIN Platform, a service infrastructure anchored《定着する》 in the relationship of trust that SECOM has cultivated《培う》 with society. Created in [Pre3]collaboration with partners who share our mission and have [Pre4]diverse technologies and expertise ([*5]"Co-Creation" strategy), this infrastructure is designed to provide peace of mind to people in their everyday lives, as well as to society as a whole.

By creating its ANSHIN Platform, SECOM aims to provide enduring《永続的な》 peace of mind to an ever-changing《常に変わりゆく》 society.

To further accelerate《加速する》 growth as we work toward achievement of our Vision for 2030, we have been advancing a variety of initiatives including creation of new services and systems and development of a [Pre5]foundation for the future, under the SECOM Group Road Map 2022. The Road Map outlines business strategies as well as human resources《人事》 and organizational strategies for both [Pre6]domestic and [Pre7]overseas markets that need to be pursued by 2022, and capital strategies《資本戦略》 including investment policies.

Going forward, through our efforts to realize the ANSHIN Platform, we aim to provide enduring peace of mind to an ever-changing society. By resolving diverse social imperatives《社会課題》, we will continue to grow together with society and achieve sustainable [Pre8]enhancement of our corporate value.

出典 https://www.secom.co.jp/english/corporate/outline/greeting/

ご家庭を見守るセコム・ホームセキュリティ

【Notes】

＊1 BPO: Business Process Outsourcing の略。効率化、生産性の向上などを目的として、データ入出力・処理業務などを外部に委託すること。

＊2 ICT: Information and Communication Technology の略。情報通信技術。

＊3 milestone: マイルストーン。路傍に置かれた道程を示す標石のことであるが、ビジネスにおいては大きな目標を達成するための重要な中間目標（ターゲット）を表す。

＊4 the ANSHIN Platform: あんしんプラットフォーム。産・官・学などのパートナーが参加して、セコムとともに暮らしや社会に安心を提供する社会インフラのこと。

＊5 “Co-Creation” Strategy: 「共想」戦略。想いを共にするパートナーとの戦略的な協働を図り、多様化する社会のニーズに応える新サービスの創出を目指す戦略。

Exercise 1

❖ Read the sentences below. Write T if the sentence is true, F if it is false.

1. (　　) The first home-security system in Japan was introduced in 1966.

2. (　　) SECOM has provided more than ten business segments in addition to their well-known security services.

3. (　　) Companies in the SECOM Group are currently found in 18 countries and territories.

4. (　　) The ANSHIN Platform is included in the SECOM Group's Vision for 2030, which will deliver peace of mind in society.

5. (　　) The SECOM Group Road Map 2022 shows future strategies to protect the global environment.

セコム株式会社

1962 年に日本初の警備会社として創業し、民放のテレビドラマ『ザ・ガードマン』のモデルとなった会社です。当初は人が主体の警備でしたが、1966 年にセンサー付きの警備システムを日本で初めて開発しました。

セコムは、1989 年に「社会システム産業」の構築を目指すことを宣言し、その実現に向かって邁進しています。「社会システム産業」とは、社会で暮らす上で、より「安心・安全」で、「快適・便利」なシステムやサービスを創造し、それらを統合・融合させ、社会になくてはならない新しい社会システムとして提供するものです。

その事業領域は、セキュリティ、防災、メディカル、保険、地理空間情報サービス、BPO･ICT、不動産事業と多岐にわたり、海外でも事業を展開。これらの事業のサービスを組み合わせたサービスの開発・提供に取り組み、いつでも、どこでも誰もが「安全・安心」で「快適・便利」に暮らせる社会の実現を目指しています。

Exercise 2

❖ Listen to the sentences and fill in the blanks.

24

1. SECOM's ( ) is to ( ) a society free from ( ).
2. The Social System Industry vision ( ) a concept of ( ) and ( ) services and systems.
3. The "SECOM brand" on-line security systems are provided with ( ) response ( ), ( ) Asia, Europe and Oceania.
4. SECOM provides ( ) services to address risks that ( ) "safety and peace of mind" in ( ) life.
5. There are increasing problems such as ( ) and accidents, natural ( ), and illness and ( ).
6. According to their ( ) philosophy, they have the duty and ( ) to always find and ( ) new businesses.
7. Fostering ( ) among employees is ( ) in order to ( ) SECOM's aim.
8. The company will act ( ) and try hard to ( ) on new potential to ( ) its operations.

Exercise 3

❖ Listen and fill in the blanks in the short conversations below. Then practice the conversations with a partner.

25

1. *Student:* What does the name "SECOM" ( ) for?

   Company: It's an ( ) of "Security Communication." The original company, Nihon Keibi Hosho Co., Ltd., was ( ) in 1962.

2. *Student:* I ( ) Nihon Keibi Hosho started a ( ) and static guard in Japan. When did your company become famous?

   Company: After ( ) security for the Olympic Village in the ( ) Tokyo Olympics, the firm received ( ) recognition and began to ( ).

3. *Student:* The ( ) of the company would have been limited only with ( ) security services. When was the first on-line security system ( )?

   Company: "SP Alarm" was developed in 1966. It ( ) monitors the premises of their ( ) 24/7 from SECOM Control Centers and ( ) immediate ( ) as needed.

Exercise 4

❖ Rearrange the words and phrases to make correct sentences.

1. セコムは顧客に安心を届けるために尽力している。
   SECOM (customers, deliver, devoted, peace, mind, its, of, is, to, to).

2. 変わりゆく世界においては、新規サービスの必要性が常に存在するであろう。
   There (a need, will, a changing, for, world, a new, be, in, service, always).

3. SECOM の基本的な理念によると、できるだけ早く行動を起こす習慣をつけることが大切である。
   According to SECOM's fundamental philosophies, it is (important, action, habit, make, take, it, a, to, to) as fast as possible.

Exercise 5

❖ Translate into English.

1. 私たちは、このビジョンに沿って（in line with）計画を推し進めるよう（push ahead with）努めます。

2. 近年における急速なテクノロジーの進化（technological advances）は、社会の変化をもたらしている。

CHAPTER 7

株式会社セブン＆アイ・ホールディングス

Seven & i Holdings Co., Ltd.

新しい便利さを提供

Pre-Reading 1 : Key Words

❖ Match each word with its definition below.

＊The words are listed in the order in which they appear in the reading.

1. synergy
2. infrastructure
3. innovator
4. underpin
5. expertise
6. collaboration
7. incorporate
8. perspective

(　　) a. the basic systems and services that are necessary for a country or an organization to run smoothly

(　　) b. to take in or contain (something) as part of a whole; include

(　　) c. special skill or knowledge

(　　) d. viewpoint; a way of seeing things

(　　) e. to form the basis for; support

(　　) f. the combined power, profits, etc. that can be achieved by two organizations or groups of people working together rather than separately

(　　) g. someone who introduces changes and new ideas

(　　) h. the situation of two or more people working together to create or achieve the same thing

Message from the President

26

Seven & i Holdings covers a globally unrivaled, diverse range of business《業》 categories《態》, including convenience stores, superstores, department stores, specialty stores, and financial services, and we have a global network of stores that includes more than 67,000 stores in total, with approximately 64 million customers, visiting our stores every day. By effectively using the Group [Pre1]synergies created by our wide range of business areas, we are able to serve as a social [Pre2]infrastructure that supports the daily lives of our customers, *[1]as well as contribute to the development of the retail services as an [Pre3]innovator.

Today, with the rapid evolution of digital technologies and the expansion of the information and communications systems that now [Pre4]underpin society, the face《姿、様相》 of retail services in Japan is changing dramatically. We are responding to these changes by working even harder than before to improve the services that we provide to our customers. By utilizing our store network and information systems that we have built up《築き上げてきた》 over the years, our business infrastructure in terms of logistics and more《～等々(＝etc.)》, our ability to offer products and services that meet the needs of customers at different life stages, and our human resources cultivation [Pre5]expertise, we are responding to these changes in Japan's retail services. In addition, we are actively working to foster [Pre6]collaboration with external experts and other companies, so as to further enrich the range of contact《接》 points《点》 with individual customers, as well as develop new markets.

We are also responding to changes in society's needs driven《引き起こされる》 by the increase in the number of working women, the trend towards low birthrate and the aging of the population, as well as the emergence of global-scale environmental issues. To do this, we are [Pre7]incorporating the environmental, social and corporate governance *[2](ESG) [Pre8]perspective into our management and business activities, and seeking《努力する》 to develop solutions《解決策を見出す》 for the problems affecting society. Furthermore, we are also making a concerted effort《協調努力》 to build new business models and new store designs《店舗設計》 that will contribute towards the realization of the United Nations' Sustainable Development Goals《持続可能な開発目標》 (SDGs) and towards the achievement of sustainable growth for society.

*[3]Going forward, the Seven & i Group will continue working as one《一丸となって》 in accordance with our Group Creed—which emphasizes the values of trust and sincerity—towards creating new value in response to the major changes

taking place in society. We will also continue to demonstrate sincerity in our relationship with customers and other stakeholders, and strive to further strengthen the relationship of trust that we have with them.

出典 https://www.7andi.com/en/company/topmsg.html

SEVEN&i HOLDINGS 株式会社セブン&アイHLDGS.

【Notes】

＊1 as well as = and also:　メディア英語では、訳し下げる意味・用法が頻繁に登場し、この本文中で出現する他の2つも同様な使われ方をしている。e.g. Black boxes are designed to withstand a tremendous impact, *as well as* deep-sea pressure and extreme temperatures. (*The New Yorker*)

＊2 ESG = environment, society and governance:　環境・社会・ガバナンス

＊3 Going forward:　今後 (= in the future; down the road)

Exercise 1

❖ Read the sentences below. Write T if the sentence is true, F if it is false.

1. (　　) Seven & i Holdings' business activities don't include financial services.

2. (　　) The company is committed to supporting customers' daily lives and developing retail services.

3. (　　) The retail services are forced to respond to the rapid and various changes in the social environment.

4. (　　) They are working to contribute to the realization of the United Nations' SDGs.

5. (　　) Their Group Creed is to aim to increase customers' level of satisfaction by putting the customer first.

株式会社セブン＆アイ・ホールディングス

国内第２位の流通グループであり、コンビニを中心に、総合スーパーではイトーヨーカドー、百貨店ではそごう西武、専門店では赤ちゃん本舗、ロフト、金融サービスではセブン銀行、フードサービスではレストランのデニーズなど、企業グループの企画・管理・運営を行っている持株会社です。特に、企業グループの稼ぎ頭はコンビニのセブン - イレブン・ジャパンであり、2019 年度において、店舗数は 71,000 を超え、客数は１日あたり 6,450 万人となっています。コンビニ発祥の地アメリカの７-Eleven, Inc. も現在傘下に入っています。国内の他、アメリカ、中国、韓国などにも店舗があり、順風満帆に発展してきたコンビニですが、他業種と同様、人手不足、コンビニ自体の飽和状態など新たな課題に立ち向かっているところです。

Exercise 2

❖ Listen to the sentences and fill in the blanks. 27

1. With a spirit of "(　　　　　　) and sincerity," the Seven & i Group strives to be a (　　　　　) business enterprise that earns the (　　　　　　) of all stakeholders.
2. Ito-Yokado's Net Supermarket (　　　　　　　) the products (　　　　　　　) by customers from nearby stores in as (　　　　　　　) as four hours.
3. You can gain "nanaco points" by (　　　　　　　) with a nanaco card at their group stores (　　　　　　　) 7-Eleven, Ito-Yokado and (　　　　　　　).
4. They are working hard to (　　　　　　) the use of additives in food products as a (　　　　) toward providing health-(　　　　　　　) products.
5. At the Denny's restaurant (　　　　　　), there is a low-allergen (　　　　　　) for children who have food (　　　　　　　).
6. The company (　　　　　　　) traceability of products as an (　　　　　　) to emphasize the (　　　　　　) and reliability of its products.
7. Convenience stores have become a (　　　　　) of Japanese culture because convenience and (　　　　　　　) are condensed in their (　　　　　) space.
8. The (　　　　　　　) in the global population and (　　　　　　　) weather have given rise to food (　　　　　　　).

Exercise 3

❖ Listen and fill in the blanks in the short conversations below. Then practice the conversations with a partner. 28

1. *Mao:* Do you know (　　　　　　) the store name "7-Eleven" means?
   Yuhto: Yes, it (　　　　　) from the old-time service (　　　　　) from 7am to 11pm.

2. *Yutaka:* I often use a nearby 7-Eleven store for (　　　　　　) shopping or to buy things late at night. On what occasion do you (　　　　　) in at convenience stores?
   Hajime: Rather than shopping, I tend to go there to pay my smartphone (　　　　) or send (　　　　　　) by home delivery service.

3. *Hitomi:* (　　　　　) is the "Seven RakuRaku Delivery" service (　　　　　)?
   Chihiro: It provides deliveries of (　　　　　) products to a customer's (　　　　　) or working place. My grandparents live in an area (　　　　　　) for daily shopping and (　　　　　　) use that service.

Exercise 4

❖ Rearrange the words and phrases to make correct sentences.

1. セブン＆アイ・ホールディングスは、災害発生時には、地域のライフラインを守り社会インフラとしての機能を果たすことに努めます。
   Seven & i Holdings (fulfill, community lifelines, of, its role, preserve, social infrastructure, to, and, strives) when disasters occur.

2. セブン - イレブン・ジャパンは、食品生産中の品質管理のレベルを改善すべく、1997 年に HACCP 方式を採用した。
   Seven-Eleven Japan adopted the HACCP method in 1997 (management, production, during, improve, quality, level, food, the, of, to).

3. 同社は 2019 年に沖縄で 14 店舗をオープンさせ、全国 47 都道府県でコンビニを展開することになった。
   In 2019, the company opened its 14 Okinawa Prefecture outlets, now (convenience stores, 47 prefectures, the country's, operating, all, in, of).

Exercise 5

❖ Translate into English.

1. その会社は、リサイクル素材（recycled materials）や生分解性素材（biodegradable materials）を使用することで、環境負荷（its environmental impact）低減に努めている（is working）。

2. コンビニには、日常生活で必要な商品やサービス（the goods and services）の大部分が揃っている（provide）。

CHAPTER 8

大正製薬ホールディングス株式会社

Taisho Pharmaceutical Holdings Co., Ltd.

「リポビタンD」で有名な製薬グループ

Pre-Reading 1 : Key Words

❖ Match each word with its definition below.

＊The words are listed in the order in which they appear in the reading.

1. responsible
2. welfare
3. circumstance
4. growth
5. overseas
6. acquire
7. restructuring
8. strengthen

(　　) a. an act of organizing a company or system in a new way to make it operate more effectively

(　　) b. financial support given to those who are unemployed or otherwise in need

(　　) c. to get or buy something

(　　) d. foreign; relating to a foreign country

(　　) e. situation; conditions

(　　) f. the process of developing or of increasing in size

(　　) g. having the duty of taking care of something

(　　) h. to make something stronger or more effective

A Message from Management

大正製薬ホールディングス／大正製薬本社

The Taisho Pharmaceutical Group《大正製薬グループ》 operates with the mission of contributing to society by creating and offering superior pharmaceuticals and health-related products as well as《and also》 healthcare-related《〜関連の》 information and services in socially [Pre1]responsible ways that enrich people's lives by improving health and beauty.

Rising social [Pre2]welfare costs have become a major problem in Japan in recent years due to the rapid shift to an aging population with a low birthrate. We believe that pharmaceutical companies have the important mission of dealing with the issues of an aging society with long life expectancy《平均寿命》.

Under these [Pre3]circumstances, Taisho Pharmaceutical Holdings Co., Ltd. (the "Company"), which is responsible for the management of the entire Group, aims to grow continuously and to strengthen competitiveness《競争力》 through the effective allocation《配分》 of business resources. We will focus on《〜に専念する》 increasing Group-wide corporate value by driving《推進する》 balanced [Pre4]growth and capturing synergies《相乗効果を生み出す》 in two broad operating areas: the Self-Medication Operation Group《セルフメディケーション事業》, which is centered on over-the-counter (OTC) drugs《一般用医薬品（市販薬）》, and the Prescription Pharmaceutical《医薬》 Operation Group《事業》, which handles ethical drugs《医療用医薬品》. By leveraging《活用する》 the strengths of each Group company and reinforcing collaboration, we are working to build a Group-wide framework《枠組み》 aimed at driving sustained《持続した》 growth.

The Company's dividend《配当金》 policy is to pay dividends largely in line with《〜にしたがって》 its consolidated business performance《連結営業実績》 each fiscal year《会計年度》, while targeting a dividend《配当性向、》 payout ratio《配当支払い率》 of 30% of net income《純利益》 excluding extraordinary income/loss《特別損益》. Barring《〜を除いて》 special circumstances, we plan to maintain an annual dividend of at least ¥100 per share《一株当たり》, even when the dividend payout ratio exceeds 30%.

In closing《最後に》, we ask for your continued understanding as we endeavor to reach our goals.

出典 https://www.taisho-holdings.co.jp/en/ir/management/message/

[pre5]
Overseas Business

30

Since [Pre6]acquiring the Asian OTC drug business of U.S.-based《米国に本社を置く》 *[1]Bristol-Myers Squibb Company in 2009, we have continued to expand our overseas OTC drug business platform with acquisitions《買収》 in Malaysia (*[2]Hoepharma) and Mexico (four companies including *[3]CICSA) and the [Pre7]restructuring of the existing joint venture《合弁事業》 in Thailand with *[4]Osotspa Co., Ltd. Total sales from the overseas OTC business (OTC drugs and energy drinks) in fiscal 2012 increased 31.3% *[5]in year-on-year terms to ¥17.6 billion, reflecting market growth and aggressive promotional activities《販売促進活動》.

In the next stage of business development, we plan to increase sales of acquired brands and develop systems to leverage the business platform created. In April 2013, the business division responsible for overseas operations was transferred from Taisho Pharmaceutical to the Company to speed up handling of regulatory matters《規制上の問題》 in each country while [Pre8]strengthening product development and the oversight《監視》 of human resources management《人材管理》 in each country.

出典 https://www.taisho-holdings.co.jp/en/business/selfmedication/overseas.html

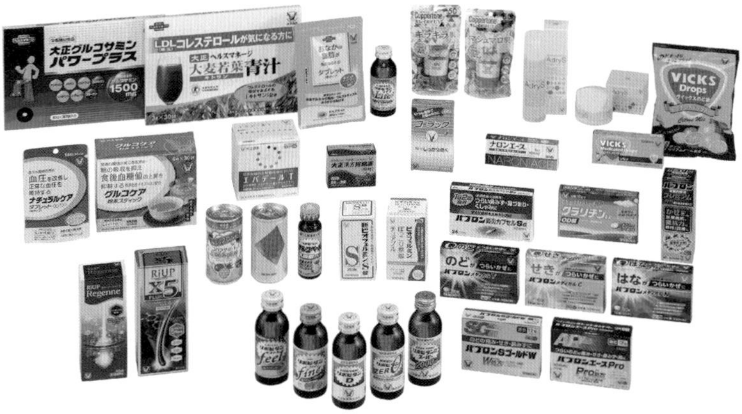

主に OTC 医薬品・食品・化粧品

【Notes】

＊1 Bristol-Myers Squibb Company:　ブリストル・マイヤーズ・スクイブ社。「バファリン」の開発で知られる、1989 年に設立されたアメリカの医薬品会社。
＊2 Hoepharma:　ホウ製薬。1979 年設立のマレーシアの医薬品会社。
＊3 CICSA:　シクサ社。メキシコの製薬グループ。
＊4 Osotspa Co., Ltd:　オソサパ株式会社。タイの飲料、消費財製品大手。
＊5 in year-on-year terms:　前年比で。in 〜 terms で「〜の観点から「すると［言えば］」の意。

Exercise 1

❖ Read the sentences below. Write T if the sentence is true, F if it is false.

1. (　　) Recently, the rapidly aging population has raised social welfare costs in Japan.

2. (　　) OTC drugs are medicines that you can get only from a doctor.

3. (　　) The Taisho Group plans to lower their annual dividend to less than ¥100 per share.

4. (　　) To expand its business abroad, the company acquired CICSA, which is a drug business company based in Malaysia.

5. (　　) The company made a major organizational change in 2013 in order to speed up its overseas operations.

大正製薬　大宮工場・研究所

大正製薬ホールディングス株式会社

　大正製薬ホールディングスを持ち株会社とする大正製薬グループは、ドリンク剤「リポビタンD」、かぜ薬「パブロン」、発毛剤「リアップ」を始めとする多くのブランドを持つ、処方箋なしに購入可能なOTC(over-the-counter) 医薬品の国内トップシェアの製薬企業グループです。国内においては、中核子会社の大正製薬が製品の販売およびマーケティングを行っています。海外でも、タイ、インドネシア、マレーシア等、東南アジアを中心にドリンク剤、OTC 医薬品等の事業を展開しています。また、医療用医薬品分野では「国際的に通用する独自の新薬開発」をテーマとし、積極的な研究開発を進め、オリジナリティの高い新薬の開発を行っています。創業大正元年 (1912 年) の大正製薬は、既に100 年を越える歴史を持ち、1963 年からドリンク剤のリポビタンシリーズで海外に進出していますが、ASEAN 諸国や中国、米国に現地法人を設立しており、今後は海外での展開を更に拡大していく予定です。

Exercise 2

Listen to the sentences and fill in the blanks.

1. Pharmaceutical companies take (   ) a greater (   ) responsibility than other (   ).
2. Longer (   ) expectancy and lower (   ) have resulted in a rapidly (   ) society.
3. We made some structural changes to (   ) our (   ) and international competitiveness.
4. To (   ) sustainable (   ) and development, more group-wide collaboration is (   ).
5. Some companies reinvest their (   ) rather than (   ) dividends to shareholders.
6. The (   ) acquisition could (   ) up the (   ) market for the company.
7. The market of OTC (   ), also known (   ) non-prescription drugs, is growing (   ).
8. Every country (   ) its own (   ) and (   ) on drugs.

Exercise 3

Listen and fill in the blanks in the short conversations below. Then practice the conversations with a partner.

1. *Student:* When (   ) your company founded?

   Company: It was (   ) founded in (   ), the year when the Taisho (   ) started.

2. *Student:* What are some of your company's most popular (   )?

   Company: We have (   )-medication brands (   ) as "Pabron," "Taisho Kampo Ichoyaku," "Colac," and the (   ) drink "Lipovitan D."

3. *Student:* Do you (   ) "Lipovitan D" (   ) Japan, too?

   Company: Yes. We also sell it in the (   ) market, but sometimes (   ) different names such as "Libogen" or "Livita," depending on the country.

Exercise 4

❖ Rearrange the words and phrases to make correct sentences.

1. 大正製薬は、顧客が信頼できる、高い価値のある製品を提供し続けています。
   Taisho Pharmaceutical Co., Ltd. (can, to, products of high value, continues, trust, that, customers, provide).

2. 私たちは、真に競争力のある新薬の開発とその継続的な発売なしには、生き残ることはできないでしょう。
   We won't be able to survive (new medicines, developing, and, truly competitive, without, continuously launching).

3. その会社は、様々なメディアを通して、自社製品の認知や理解を促進しています。
   The company is promoting (their products, the recognition, various types, understanding, through, media, and, of, of).

Exercise 5

❖ Translate into English.

1. リポビタンDは、日本のエナジードリンク市場で圧倒的なシェア（a dominant share）を誇っている。

2. その会社の各製品に関する詳細な（detailed）説明は、ウェブサイト上で、確認することができる。

CHAPTER 9

東レ株式会社

Toray Industries, Inc.

素材には、社会を変える力がある

Pre-Reading 1 : Key Words

❖ Match each word with its definition below.

＊The words are listed in the order in which they appear in the reading.

1 . inception
2 . firm
3 . spark
4 . advent
5 . challenge
6 . application
7 . affect
8 . underlie

(　　) a. to have an influence on something or someone
(　　) b. a difficult task or problem
(　　) c. a way in which something can be used for a particular purpose
(　　) d. beginning; start
(　　) e. to give rise to; lead to
(　　) f. to be the foundation, cause, or basis of something
(　　) g. definite and not likely to change
(　　) h. emergence; appearance; arrival

Advanced Materials Give Shape to Advanced Industries

33

Since its very [Pre1]inception, the Toray Group has continuously carried out research and development on advanced materials《先端材料》 based on the [Pre2]firm conviction that research and technology development provide the key to building the Toray of tomorrow. Materials have a low profile《目立たない存在》 because they are hidden in the final product, but history attests to《～を証明[立証]する》 the fact that advanced materials have created next-generation industries. For example, the invention of synthetic polymers《合成高分子[ポリマー]》 [Pre3]sparked the creation of numerous industries including today's synthetic fiber and plastic industries. Similarly, the discovery of semiconductors led to transistors, LSI《大規模集積回路》, and the modern IT industry. Today, a new aircraft industry is developing thanks to the [Pre4]advent of carbon fiber《炭素繊維》 composite materials《複合材料》. In order to provide true solutions to the many societal and economic [Pre5]challenges of our times, there is no other way than the pursuit of technology and material innovation. Without such innovation, there can never be final products that are attractive to the market.

東レ株式会社

Persistent efforts based on insight into material value

34

It inevitably takes a certain amount of time to develop and commercialize《商品化する》 a material. As an example, Toray began research on carbon fibers in 1961. Commercial production began 10 years later in 1971, and today these fibers are used in numerous aircraft, such as the Boeing 787. Many overseas chemical companies withdrew from development of carbon fibers or scaled down their efforts, but Toray saw their potential value as a material, and worked persistently, developing the business through [Pre6]applications in fishing rods and golf shafts, while looking toward《～を見据える》 aircraft applications in the long-term. This ability to see the value of materials and the strong will to follow through《とことん追求する》 are the strengths of Toray's R&D, and the backdrop《背景》 which gives rise to genuine innovation. In addition, our management provides continuous R&D investment, without being [Pre7]affected by the ups and downs of the economic climate《景気、経済状況》, and for many years we have made no major changes in R&D expenditures《支出》 as a percentage of sales. These points also demonstrate the commitment of Toray's R&D to distant《どこまでも遠い》 long-term continuity.

The DNA of Toray researchers and engineers: The Deeper, the Newer

The phrase, [*1]"The Deeper, the Newer," has been passed down as a key phrase at Toray, and is part of the DNA of our researchers and engineers. The concept [Pre8]underlying this is that when you dig deep into《～を深く掘り下げる》 something, the result will be new discoveries and inventions. We are always in pursuit of the ultimate limits. This pursuit of R&D cannot be achieved with a complacent《独り善がりの》 attitude《態度》; it has to be based on a grand vision of the times and the needs of society. Only then can we create genuine innovation that has value to society and the economy.

出典 2019 年の東レ株式会社 Web ページより転載

未来創造研究センター

【Notes】

＊1 "The Deeper, the Newer": 「深は新なり」。'the+ 比較級 , the+ 比較級 ' の構文で、「～すればするほど、ますます……」の意。e.g. The sooner (it is), the better (it is). / The older you grow, the weaker your memory becomes.

Exercise 1

❖ Read the sentences below. Write T if the sentence is true, F if it is false.

1. (　　) Historically, advanced materials have helped set up next-generation industries.

2. (　　) It is not technology but material innovation that gives birth to attractive final products.

3. (　　) The development of carbon fibers has been continued by chemical companies worldwide.

4. (　　) Toray's ability and willingness to see the value of materials has led to genuine innovation.

5. (　　) Toray believes that complacency is inseparable from the ultimate pursuit of R&D.

東レ株式会社

東レ株式会社は1926年、レーヨン糸の生産会社としてスタートしました。以来、基礎素材メーカーとして、新分野・新素材の開拓に励み、創業時の繊維に加えて、樹脂、ケミカル、フィルム、さらには炭素繊維複合材料、電子情報材料、医薬・医療、水処理・環境といった様々な分野において多くの先端材料、高付加価値製品を創出してきました。ものづくりの中核である日本国内で創出した高付加価値製品の用途開発を世界各地で行うことにより、グローバルな規模での持続的な成長サイクルを実現しています。「企業の社会的責任」を重んじ、「安全・防災・環境保全」並びに「企業倫理・法令遵守」を最優先の経営課題に位置づけるとともに、社会に役立つ製品・サービスを提供することで、ステークホルダーの皆様の期待に応えています。

Exercise 2

❖ Listen to the sentences and fill in the blanks. 36

1. At the Toray Group, they consider ( ) to be the most ( ) global ( ) of the 21st century.
2. Toray works to ( ) the world's ( ) on fossil fuel resources by ( ) plant-based fibers.
3. Every product people ( ) is made from materials, and we believe ( ) can change ( ).
4. Starting from ( ) filament businesses, the Toray Group is now a manufacturer of ( ) major synthetic fibers; polyester, ( ) and acrylic fiber.
5. Carbon-fiber ( ) are used in products ( ) from bicycles to Formula One cars and from wind turbines to ( ) cases.
6. Global carbon-fiber ( ) is expected to more than ( ) from 60,000 tons in 2015 to around ( ) tons in 2025.
7. A chemical giant, Toray specializes in ( ) products such as synthetic ( ) and ( ), and information-related materials.
8. The ( ) drive to build a more sustainable world would be ( ) without the ( ) industry.

Exercise 3

❖ Listen and fill in the blanks in the short conversations below. Then practice the conversations with a partner. 37

1. *Student:* What is the ( ) of your company name?

   Company: "TO" ( ) for "TO" of "TOYO" or the Japanese for the East, and "RAY" for "RAY" of "RAYON." Toray, formerly known as Toyo ( ) Co., Ltd., was founded in 1926 as a rayon filament manufacturer.

2. *Student:* What kind of ( ) does the Toray Group make?

   Company: We at the Toray Group are ( ) involved in manufacturing ( ). Our products and materials can be found in various ( ).

3. *Student:* What is the Corporate ( ) of the Toray Group?

   Company: It is "Contributing to society through the ( ) of new value with innovative ideas, ( ) and ( )."

Exercise 4

❖ Rearrange the words and phrases to make correct sentences.

1. 東レ株式会社は、革新技術を通じて、先端材料で世界のトップ企業になることを目指している。
   Toray Industries, Inc. (advanced materials, top company, become, innovation, through, global, aims, to, of, a).

2. 東レは、航空機や自動車の軽量化が図れる軽くて強い炭素繊維を提供している。
   Toray (lightweight and strong, carbon fiber, the weight, provides, reduce, that, can, of) aircraft and automobiles.

3. 炭素繊維は、鉄の重さの 4 分の 1 でありながら、強度は 10 倍もあります。
   Carbon fiber offers (a quarter, the strength, steel, times, just, for, ten, of) of its weight.

Exercise 5

❖ Translate into English.

1. 炭素繊維は、強さと軽さ・耐久性（durability）を持つ（offer）限られた（few）素材の 1 つです。

2. 東レは、私たち日々の生活に密接に（intimately）関わる（involved in）多くの製品を生み出してきました。

CHAPTER 10

豊田通商株式会社

Toyota Tsusho Corporation

トヨタグループの総合商社

Pre-Reading 1 : Key Words

❖ Match each word with its definition below.

＊The words are listed in the order in which they appear in the reading.

1. surrounding
2. domain
3. prosperous
4. stakeholder
5. humbly
6. overall
7. given
8. optimize

(　　) a. area; field
(　　) b. as a whole; in general
(　　) c. considering; taking into account
(　　) d. to make something as good or as effective as possible
(　　) e. near or around something
(　　) f. bringing wealth and success
(　　) g. a person or group of people who own a share in a business
(　　) h. in a way that shows you do not consider yourself as better than others

Message from the President & CEO

38

Upon assuming the office of president & CEO from April 1, 2018, please let me share with you my aspirations.

With rapid advances in technology, such as in the form of AI and [*1]IoT, industry today is facing a time of monumental《very big; enormous》 structural transformation. It changes significantly in the [Pre1]surrounding business environment, including in our chief business [Pre2]domain of [*2]Mobility. [*3]Viewing that such environmental changes bring not only risk but also opportunity, I intend to harness《利用する》 the situation for the creation of new business models that are in harmony with society.

At the same time, while《～しながら(も)》 never forgetting the Toyota Tsusho [*4]Group Way, which is the DNA of our company—in other words, "A Passion for Business," [*5]"On-Site, Hands-On, In-Touch" and "Teamwork," and other elements that make our company what it is《現在[今日]の姿》, I would like to unite with the employees of the entire Toyota Tsusho Group and create new value, aiming to be a company that contributes to the building of a [Pre3]prosperous future for all.

Our company greeted its 70th anniversary on July 1, 2018. I would like to sincerely express my deep appreciation to all [Pre4]stakeholders who have supported our development thus far《これまで》. And I [Pre5]humbly request that they will continue to provide us with their encouragement and guidance.

出典 https://www.toyota-tsusho.com/english/company/message.html

39

Striving《～に向けて努力する》 for Medium- and Long-term Development Led by the [*6]Africa Division

Africa is a continent with tremendous capacity《潜在的発展[成長]の可能性》 and potential《将来性》. It has been called the final frontier. This is due in part to its rapidly expanding middle class and its growing and youthful population. While there are African countries that struggle with《～に苦しむ、と戦う》 political instability, deficits《財政赤字》, and tribal《種族の、部族の》 conflicts,

in recent years the foundation of democracy has made progress [Pre6]overall, and stable economic growth is now expected. Another reason that the world's attention is turning to Africa is that its population is growing rapidly, and it has high potential as a commercial market due to rising consumption by the middle class.

[Pre7]Given this background, Toyota Tsusho, which is engaging in business in Africa with a medium- and long-term perspective, established the Africa Division in April 2017 to integrate《統合する》 its Africa-related business. It is made up of four strategic business units(SBUs)《戦略的事業ユニット（SBU）》: the Mobility SBU, which is developing business by leveraging《活用する》 a sales network covering the entire continent; the Healthcare SBU, which aims to expand business based on [*7]CFAO's 70-year track record《実績》 in pharmaceutical wholesaling《卸売り》 in Africa; the Consumer Goods SBU, which is engaged in local production and retailing《小売り（活動）》 of consumer goods such as beverages and ballpoint pens; and the Technology & Energy SBU, which is promoting renewable energy and the harbor development business. The division has unified《一本化[一体化]する》 the chain of command《指揮［命令］系統》 involved in strategies and investment, with the aim of [Pre8]optimizing all business in Africa.

出典 https://www.toyota-tsusho.com/english/about/project/19/

【Notes】

＊1 IoT = Internet of Things: 「モノのインターネット」。インターネットに様々な機器や装置をつなげ、相互に情報伝達できるようになることを意味する。
＊2 Mobility: 移動利便性。この文中では、「自動車、自動車関連事業」の意味。
＊3 Viewing that: ～であるから、～なので。なお、Seeing that の方が一般的である。
＊4 Group Way: グループの基本理念、行動指針。
＊5 "On-Site, Hands-On, In-Touch": 「現地･現物･現実」。「現地に足を運び、現物を見て、現実を直視した上で、常に原理･原則に則り、自分の目で正しい判断を行う。」という豊田通商グループウェイの１つ。
＊6 Africa Division: アフリカ本部。豊田通商株式会社は、2012 年にフランスの商社 CFAO へ資本参加し、2016 年には同社を完全子会社化し、2017 年にアフリカ関連の事業を統合・集約し、アフリカ本部を新設した。
＊7 CFAO = Cie. Française de l'Afrique Occidentale SAS。1887 年創業の西アフリカを中心に活動しているフランス商社の略称

Exercise 1

❖ Read the sentences below. Write T if the sentence is true, F if it is false.

1. (　　) Industry is now experiencing a lot of structural changes.

2. (　　) The president and CEO hopes to build a prosperous future for the workers of the whole group of Toyota Tsusho.

3. (　　) While people in Africa might be in a bad political or financial situation, some of them are enjoying buying more things than before.

4. (　　) The African Division is composed of the Mobility SBU, the Healthcare SBU and Technology & Energy SBU.

5. (　　) The African Division is trying to find ways to improve all its business in Africa.

豊田通商株式会社

国内および海外 120 カ国以上におよぶグローバルネットワークと、500 社を超える連結グループ会社を通じ、事業を展開している総合商社です。「金属本部」「グローバル部品・ロジスティクス本部」「自動車本部」「機械・エネルギー・プラントプロジェクト本部」「化学品・エレクトロニクス本部」「食料・生活産業本部」「アフリカ本部」の 7 本部体制で、幅広い事業領域をカバーしています。

最近のプロジェクトでは、地熱発電建設を通じ、ケニアの経済成長を支援しています。地熱発電は、火山帯の地下にあるマグマによって熱せられた高温・高圧の地下水（蒸気）を利用して発電を行うため、天候や時間帯に左右されることなく安定的に電力を供給できるのが大きな特長です。完工した発電所の総発電量はアフリカでも最大で、ケニア国内の総発電量の約 20％を安定的に供給することができます。電力インフラの他、農業、ICT など、アフリカの課題解決につながる分野で、新規事業に取り組んでいます。

Exercise 2

❖ Listen to the sentences and fill in the blanks. 40

1. The general trading company business model ( ) on two axes— ( ) and business ( ).
2. All corporate ( ) are ( ) by social trust and sustained by social ( ).
3. Toyota Tsusho Corporation plans to ( ) their business and ( ) the growth in Africa around ( ) business.
4. The company strives to ( ) impact on the environment, conserve energy, ( ) resources and eliminate environmental ( ).
5. Countries in every ( ) of the world are turning to renewable energy as the ( ) to reducing their environmental footprint and diversifying ( ).
6. Africa has been called the "last ( )" because ( ) its abundant natural ( ) and emerging middle class.
7. Geothermal power ( ) are powered by hot, highly pressurized ( ) water heated by magma under the Earth's ( ) zone.
8. To expand the ( ) in Africa, they plan to contribute to the ( ) development of African society ( ) their business.

Exercise 3

❖ Listen and fill in the blanks in the short conversations below. Then practice the conversations with a partner. 41

1. *Company:* Have you ever ( ) of Toyota Tsusho's business in ( )?
   Student: Of ( ) I have. I know your company built a geothermal ( ) plant in the Republic of ( ).

2. *Student:* Why do you ( ) your business in Africa?
   Company: Well, there are plenty of ( ) left untouched there. It is believed that Africa is the ( ) area with big business ( ) in the world.

3. *Student:* In how many African ( ) do you conduct your ( )?
   Company: We operate in ( ) regional economic ( ) out of 54 African ( ).

Exercise 4

❖ Rearrange the words and phrases to make correct sentences.

1. 豊田通商株式会社は、国内および海外 120 カ国以上に及ぶグローバルネットワークを通じ、世界中の顧客とビジネスを展開している。
   Toyota Tsusho Corporation (a global network, across the world, customers, business, conducts, covering, through, Japan, with) and more than120 other countries.

2. 2012 年に、その会社はアフリカを中心に自動車や医薬品を取り扱うフランスの商社へ資本参画しました。
   In 2012, the company (automotive, investment, French, a capital, made, and, in, a) pharmaceutical trading company focused on Africa.

3. 急激な市場変化に迅速に対応するための戦略的取り組みは、会社が着実に成長するために極めて重要です。
   The strategic initiatives (market changes, response, sudden, rapid, essential, are, for, to) for the company to grow steadily.

Exercise 5

❖ Translate into English.

1. その会社は、豊かな（prosperous）社会づくりに貢献する価値創造組織（value-generating organization）であることを目指しています。

2. 私たちは社会的に責任を負い、地球環境の保全（conservation）に努める（strive for）べきです。

CHAPTER 11

日清食品ホールディングス株式会社

NISSIN FOODS HOLDINGS CO., LTD.

EARTH FOOD CREATOR

Pre-Reading 1 : Key Words

❖ Match each word with its definition below.

＊The words are listed in the order in which they appear in the reading.

1 . turbulent
2 . beneficial
3 . mainstay
4 . shelf-life
5 . sanitary
6 . nutritional
7 . assurance
8 . pursuit

(　　) a. a positive declaration intended to give confidence
(　　) b. a thing on which something else is based or depends
(　　) c. characterized by conflict, disorder or confusion
(　　) d. relating to the substances in food that help you stay healthy
(　　) e. the length of time for which an item, especially food, can be kept before it becomes too old to sell or use
(　　) f. favorable; advantageous
(　　) g. the act of trying to achieve a situation
(　　) h. hygienic and clean

Celebrating Our 60th Anniversary

42

安藤百福

The year 2018 marked the 60th anniversary of the founding of NISSIN FOOD PRODUCTS, or in other words《言い換えれば》, the 60-year milestone《里程標、節目》 since the invention of instant noodles. The company founder, Momofuku Ando, who lived through the [Pre1]turbulent years of [*1]both world wars, developed Chicken Ramen, the world's first instant noodles, at the age of 48 out of the desire to do something [Pre2]beneficial for people and to engage in work that would make the world a better place. The reason that, 60 years after its introduction, Chicken Ramen remains one of our popular [Pre3]mainstay products is that the founder thought through his solution to a difficult problem—how to create a product that consumers truly want and that people would find convenient.

In developing Chicken Ramen, Ando set five objectives: instant noodles must taste delicious, they must have a long [Pre4]shelf-life, they must be quick and easy to prepare, they must be inexpensive, and they must be safe and [Pre5]sanitary. Since instant noodles are a food product, safety and taste are especially important. However, in addition to satisfying these basic requirements, Ando developed "magic ramen" that required no cooking or addition of a separate broth《別添スープ》 and could be prepared in just three minutes by adding hot water.

チキンラーメン（1958）

チキンラーメン

Ando often said, "I'm not selling noodles. I'm providing time to our customers." From the moment it was created, Chicken Ramen was an exceptional food《絶品フード》 that reflected consideration for the Earth's sustainability《持続可能性》 with its ability to save《節約する、省く》 time, energy, and resources.

43

Realizing Ultimate Deliciousness through Safety, Peace of Mind, and Enjoyment

The most important function of food products is the [Pre6]nutritional function that sustains life. However, meals taken solely for the sake of subsistence《生きていくために》 are seldom delicious nor enjoyable. [Pre7]Assurance of food safety and the ability to enjoy meals with peace of mind《安心》 contributes to ultimate《究極の》 deliciousness.

Since its founding, NISSIN FOODS PRODUCTS has considered the [Pre8]pursuit of food safety the most important management priority. We develop products that consumers can enjoy with confidence《信頼》 and peace of mind through measures such as introducing pharmaceutical-level safety standards《医薬品レベルの安全基準》 in product quality management. Entertainment value is also necessary for making food products appealing. The NISSIN FOODS Group will provide enjoyment to consumers through unique marketing under the policy "What isn't enjoyable isn't delicious."

出典 NISSIN FOODS GROUP SUSTAINABILITY REPORT 2018, Message from the CEO (p.02-03)

【Notes】

＊1 both world wars: 第一次世界大戦と第二次世界大戦のこと。

Exercise 1

❖ Read the sentences below. Write T if the sentence is true, F if it is false.

1. (　　) The company "NISSIN FOODS PRODUCTS" was founded in 1958.

2. (　　) Momofuku Ando invented instant noodles during the second world war.

3. (　　) Momofuku Ando wanted instant noodles to be kept for a long period.

4. (　　) The soup for Chicken Ramen is packaged separately.

5. (　　) It is impossible to satisfy both safety and good taste of instant noodles.

カップヌードル　発売当時

カップヌードル　レギュラー

日清食品ホールディングス株式会社

同社は世界初のインスタントラーメン「チキンラーメン」や「カップヌードル」などの即席麺の製造および販売を事業とする日清食品を中心とする、日清食品グループの持株会社です。

日清食品グループは、日清食品創業者の安藤百福が掲げた「食足世平」「食創為世」「美健賢食」「食為聖職」の4つの精神をもとに、世の中のために食を創造することを追求し、日々、Creative で Unique な仕事に取り組み、Global な領域で、「食」を通じて世界の人々に Happy を提供することで、グループ理念である「EARTH FOOD CREATOR」の体現を目指しています。また、総合食品企業グループとして、各カテゴリーの中で常に No. 1 ブランドを創造・育成していき、No.1 ブランドの集合体として形成される「ブランディングコーポレーション」の実現を目指しています。

Exercise 2

Listen to the sentences and fill in the blanks.

1. The NISSIN FOODS Group (　　　　　　) various (　　　　　　　　) for food and creates dream-inspiring delicious (　　　　　　).
2. The company (　　　　　　　　) to society and the earth by (　　　　　　　　) people everywhere with pleasures and (　　　　　　) food can provide.
3. According to a UN estimate, the world (　　　　　　　　) will reach 10 billion in 2055, and there is the (　　　　　　) of a worldwide food (　　　　　　).
4. If the (　　　　　　) of food is disrupted, a country is (　　　　　　) to decline and (　　　　　　) invariably occurs.
5. The business (　　　　　　　　) of the NISSIN FOODS Group (　　　　　　　　) from the spirit of the (　　　　　　　　): "Peace will come to the world when there is enough food."
6. The company is also creating a new food (　　　　　　) and (　　　　　　　　) people all over the world with happiness and (　　　　　　　　).
7. The desire to satisfy (　　　　　　　　) and the taste buds is a common human (　　　　　　　　). However, food is also important for forming strong bodies and (　　　　　　　　　) health.
8. NISSIN "Cup Noodle," launched in (　　　　　　), is Japan's No. 1 (　　　　　　　　) and the first cup-(　　　　　　) instant noodles in the world.

Exercise 3

Listen and fill in the blanks in the short conversations below. Then practice the conversations with a partner.

1. *Student:* I heard that Momofuku Ando had a hard time (　　　　　　　　) instant noodles.

   Company: Yes, he spent day after day preparing and (　　　　　　　　) countless (　　　　　　) products.

2. *Student:* Did Chicken Ramen become popular as soon as it was (　　　　　　) in the market?

   Company: Actually not. The (　　　　　　) of wholesalers were (　　　　　　) to stock Chicken Ramen because it was (　　　　　　　　).

3. *Student:* How did it become a hit product?

   Company: It gained a (　　　　　　　　　) among the people who actually ate it. They found it tasty and (　　　　　　　　　) before wholesalers started to (　　　　　　) a lot of it.

Exercise 4

❖ Rearrange the words and phrases to make correct sentences.

1. 長期保存と簡便性の実現は、安藤百福がチキンラーメンの開発で直面した最も高い壁だった。
   Achieving (was, preservability, the, barrier, convenience, and, highest) that Momofuku Ando faced in developing Chicken Ramen.

2. リップマークは日清食品グループの象徴です。「食」を楽しむ人の口元、「食」を通して広がっていく笑顔、「食」にかかせない器を表現しています。
   The Lip Logo is a symbol of the NISSIN FOODS Group, and it (a person, on, “food”, enjoys, of, represents, through, the mouth shape, “food”, a big smile, who, their face) and a bowl for “food.”

3. チキンラーメンは、日本において共稼ぎ世帯の数が増えはじめた時期に発売された。
   Chicken Ramen went on sale at a time (in Japan, increase, when, households, to, the number, began, double-income, of).

Exercise 5

❖ Translate into English.

1. 戦後、通りは空腹な人々であふれ（be filled with）、多くが栄養失調（malnutrition）で亡くなった。

2. 瞬間油熱乾燥法（the flash-frying method）が、お湯を加えるだけで麺を食べられる状態にした（make noodles ready）。

CHAPTER 12

株式会社ファーストリテイリング

FAST RETAILING CO., LTD.

「ユニクロ」を世界展開

Pre-Reading 1 : Key Words

Match each word with its definition below.

*The words are listed in the order in which they appear in the reading.

1. proud
2. fuel
3. lasting
4. emerging
5. crave
6. distribute
7. era
8. like-minded

( ) a. to have a very strong desire for (something)
( ) b. feeling pride
( ) c. having similar opinions and interests
( ) d. existing or continuing for a long time
( ) e. to supply (goods) to retailers
( ) f. age; a period of time
( ) g. becoming apparent; starting to exist
( ) h. to support or stimulate; encourage

LifeWear is changing our world

46

I'm really [Pre1]proud of Fast Retailing's achievement of yet another record performance in FY2019. I believe the key factor [Pre2]fueling these buoyant《上向きの》 results is the strong affinity《親近感》 consumers worldwide feel for our simple but ingenious《工夫を凝らした》, high-quality LifeWear everyday clothing that is designed to make all our lives better. This is especially true in the Asian markets of Japan, Greater China (Mainland China, Hong Kong and Taiwan) and Southeast Asia & Oceania, where UNIQLO has established an overwhelmingly strong brand position. And now, the UNIQLO brand is also gaining wider support among customers in Europe and North America as well.

Where is this growing global support for our LifeWear values coming from? I believe it stems from growing doubts and a general malaise《漠然とした不安感》 towards mass consumption models of society. Today, as many events bring the [Pre3]lasting prosperity of the human race into question, people are demanding a better solution and a new style of everyday living. With apparel too, people are growing more aware of the problems associated with buying clothes to wear just a few times, and are increasingly interested in simple, high-quality, high-functioning everyday clothing. UNIQLO LifeWear epitomizes《典型的に表す》 the ultimate everyday clothing that this [Pre4]emerging society [Pre5]craves by striving to satisfy carefully considered essential《不可欠な》 everyday life needs.

We have also made great progress on our Ariake Project to reform our entire supply chain and change our employee working patterns, and we are starting to see the benefits of our campaign slogan to "make, [Pre6]distribute and sell only what is necessary." I believe pursuing our [*1]Ariake Project is the surest way to contribute to the realization of a sustainable society, to which we, as a Group, are wholeheartedly committed.

In today's [Pre7]era, every single company and every single individual must change the way they think and act to focus on developing sustainable practices. We at Fast Retailing intend to do everything we can to join forces with《～と力を合わせる》 [Pre8]like-minded companies and individuals to help create a new and better society.

November 2019
Tadashi Yanai
Chairman, President and CEO

出典 https://www.fastretailing.com/eng/ir/direction/message.html

【Notes】

＊1 Ariake Project: 有明プロジェクト。世界中の人々に Lifewear を提供するため、社員全員の働き方を根本から変え、商品の企画・計画・生産・物流・販売の総てのサプライチェーンを改革するプロジェクト。2017 年春から開始。

Exercise 1

❖ Read the sentences below. Write T if the sentence is true, F if it is false.

1. (　　) The sales of Fast Retailing reached a record high in FY2019.

2. (　　) The UNIQLO brand has enjoyed widespread popularity in Europe and North America rather than in the Asian countries.

3. (　　) There is a growing tendency for people to be reluctant to purchase disposable clothes that they wear a couple of times and throw away.

4. (　　) UNIQLO LifeWear clothing is designed to make everyone's life much happier and more luxurious.

5. (　　) The Ariake Project aims to fundamentally revolutionize the entire supply chain and change the way all the employees work.

株式会社ファーストリテイリング

カジュアル衣料専門店「ユニクロ」を中心に世界展開しているアパレル会社で、今では「ＧＵ（ジーユー）」が第２の柱になっています。商品企画・生産・物流・販売まで一貫して行う SPA（speciality store retailer of private label apparel アパレル製造小売企業）のビジネスモデルを確立し、高品質なカジュアルを手頃な価格で提供することで、飛躍的な成長を続けています。海外進出は 2001 年からスタートし、中国、韓国、アメリカ、フィリピン、タイ、マレーシアなど世界 24 の国と地域で、ユニクロだけで 1,421 店舗（2020 年 5 月現在）を展開しています。2019 年 8 月期の売上高は 2 兆 2,905 億円で、売上比率は、国内ユニクロ 38%、海外ユニクロ 45%、ジーユー 10%、グローバルブランド 7%となります。柳井社長の強力なリーダーシップのもと、経済環境に順応した迅速な運営に定評があり、海外の売上げが飛躍的に伸びています。本社は山口県山口市にあります。

Exercise 2

❖ Listen to the sentences and fill in the blanks. 47

1. Fast Retailing strives to enhance people's (　　　　) and (　　　　) living through the (　　　　) of clothes.
2. (　　　　) at more affordable prices and (　　　　) at younger clients, GU has become one of the growth (　　　　) of Fast Retailing on its own merits.
3. We will continue to (　　　　) to society through a truly great (　　　　) business that offers new and unique (　　　　).
4. Around 90% of UNIQLO's manufacturing is (　　　　) in China, Vietnam, Indonesia, Bangladesh, Turkey and India—(　　　　) its production offices are (　　　　).
5. Japanese (　　　　) apparel retailer, UNIQLO (　　　　) its first ever (　　　　) in New Delhi, India, on October 4, 2019.
6. Corporate (　　　　) can suddenly ruin the (　　　　) of a brand that has (　　　　) years to build.
7. Environmental pollution from plastic (　　　　) is a growing (　　　　) worldwide, and Fast Retailing has taken action to (　　　　) unnecessary single-use plastic from its operations.
8. Fast Retailing plans on selling new (　　　　) made from (　　　　) plastic (　　　　) and down jackets.

Exercise 3

❖ Listen and fill in the blanks in the short conversations below. Then practice the conversations with a partner. 48

1. *Student:* What does your company name Fast Retailing (　　　　)?
   Company: The English words FAST and RETAILING are (　　　　) because we want to both (　　　　) to and fulfill our customers' needs (　　　　).

2. *Student:* What is the (　　　　) behind UNIQLO's low prices?
   Company: We can (　　　　) customers low-priced apparel because we are in (　　　　) of the entire process—from the making to the (　　　　) of our products.

3. *Student:* What is UNIQLO's best-selling (　　　　)?
   Company: Might it be our fleece products? No, actually, it is our HEATTECH (　　　　). Since its (　　　　) in 2003, we have (　　　　) over 1 billion HEATTECH items worldwide.

Exercise 4

❖ Rearrange the words and phrases to make correct sentences.

1. 株式会社ファーストリテイリングは、世界中の人々に服を着るという体験を楽しく満足のいくものにすることを目指しているグローバル企業です。
   FAST RETAILING CO., LTD. is a global corporation (experience, wearing, clothes, seeking, make, the, of, to) a joyous and satisfying one.

2. 年中最も心地よく着用できるインナーウェアのエアリズムは、汗や熱を発散させ、暑い夏の期間中でも、肌をフレッシュで乾いた状態に保ちます。
   The most comfortable year-round innerwear, AIRism (fresh and dry, moisture, exhales, keeps, your, heat, skin, and, and) even during a hot summer.

3. ファーストリテイリングは、環境問題に取り組むべく、買い物袋をプラスチックから紙製に変えて有料化し始めました。
   Fast Retailing has started (shopping bags, switching, charging, plastic, paper, them, from, and, for, to) to tackle environmental issues.

Exercise 5

❖ Translate into English.

1. LifeWear は、誰にでも手が届く(everyone can afford)価格の、究極の普段着です。

2. 徹底した（comprehensive）品質と安全の管理が、安心（secure）で安全な商品を顧客に届けるために必要とされます。

CHAPTER 13

株式会社安川電機

YASKAWA Electric Corporation

産業用ロボットを製造

Pre-Reading 1 : Key Words

❖ Match each word with its definition below.

＊The words are listed in the order in which they appear in the reading.

1 . value
2 . solution
3 . maintain
4 . revolutionary
5 . expectation
6 . shortage
7 . utilize
8 . competitive

(　　) a. a hope that something good will happen
(　　) b. a situation in which there is not enough of something
(　　) c. as good as or better than others at the same level or standard
(　　) d. completely different from what was done before
(　　) e. to use something in an effective way
(　　) f. the answer to a problem
(　　) g. the importance, worth or usefulness of something
(　　) h. to make something continue

Message from Hiroshi Ogasawara

As a 'technology-centric'《technology-centered 技術を中核とした》 company aiming to be the world's best, Yaskawa achieves sustainable growth while providing new [Pre1]values to customers through a new [Pre2]solution concept, 'i^3-[*1]Mechatronics.'

Since being founded in 1915, Yaskawa Electric has set 'electric motors and their applications《応用》' as its business domain《ビジネス分野》 and supported the leading-edge《最先端の》 industries of the age. In order to engage in《～に携わる》 business with its own technology, the company established a creed of 'becoming a technology-centered《技術を中核とした》 company,' proposed the concept of 'mechatronics' ahead of the rest of the world, and has [Pre3]maintained quality-first management with the determination《決意》 to develop the world's first-in-class《そのクラスで最高の》 and [Pre4]revolutionary technologies and products. Yaskawa's core technologies are 'motion control《モーション制御》,' 'robotics《ロボット工学》,' and 'power conversion《パワー変換》.' These technologies and products born and created out of our search for elaborate control of mechanical movements contribute on a daily basis《日常的に》 to improvements in the quality and efficiency《効率》 of manufacturing《ものづくり》 around the world.

ロボットがロボットを作る生産ライン

Our business hubs《拠点》 are located in 30 countries around the world including Japan, and the production bases are located in 12 countries. We operate a [*2]glocal business which is adapted to each region's characteristics. Yaskawa's technologies, products and services are enjoying high reputation and great trust from customers worldwide.

In recent years, [Pre5]expectations for our solutions provided with servos《servomotors》 and robots have been increasing in response to challenges such as automation《自動化》 or labor saving《省人化》 against the backdrop of《～を背景に》 workforce [Pre6]shortage and rise of labor cost《人件費》 mainly in China. With the industrial advancement, manufacturing industries all over the world are undergoing rapid changes including the realization of [*3]Industrie4.0, the utilization of [*4]Internet of Things (IoT) or Artificial Intelligence (AI)《人工知能(AI)》.

Under such conditions, we launched《始動させる》 a new solution concept 'i^3-Mechatronics' in October 2017 to realize the new industrial automation revolution put forward《提示された》 in the long-term management plan '[*5]Vision 2025.' 'I^3 (iCube)' stands for《～を表す》 three 'i's of integrated《総合的》, intelligent《知能的》 and innovative《革新的》. In addition to our current

株式会社安川電機本社

state-of-the-art《最先端の》 solutions using servos, AC drives《インバータ》 and robots, we provide digital data solutions with software to realize; 1) improvement of productivity by [Pre7]utilizing operational data《運用データ》 from machinery and equipment, 2) securing and maintaining of high quality, and 3) zero-downtime《稼働停止時間のない》 production by means of《～を用いて》 failure prognosis《故障予知》 of equipment using AI.

In 2018, we released a digital data management tool《ソフトウェアツール》 'YASKAWA Cockpit,' which is the core of 'i^3-Mechatronics.' With this tool, which allows us to collect and visualize《可視化する》 data of devices from production sites as well as《and also》 to accumulate and analyze data in a comprehensive manner《包括的に、総合的に》, we provide digital data solutions defined in 'i^3-Mechatronics', and support the advancement of manufacturing of our customers.

Moreover, in autumn 2018, Yaskawa Solution Factory, which is a next-generation production factory that utilizes IoT and AI, was established within Iruma Plant in Saitama Prefecture, the mother factory of a motion control business, and we began the production of 'Σ-7 Series,' the primary product of the AC servo drive. Our customers have a great expectation for 'i^3-Mechatronics,' and we strive to《～するよう努力する》 promote the solution and our business activities for a further expansion《更なる拡大のために》.

Yaskawa endeavors to《～しようと努める》 create new value for our customers by proposing solutions that combine [Pre8]competitive hardware and software. At the same time, in order to emphasize our business values sustainably《持続的に》, we continue providing more values together with our stakeholders《利害関係者》 including business partners, shareholders《株主》, investors《投資家》, communities, employees, and so on.

出典 https://www.yaskawa.co.jp/company/profile/message

【Notes】

＊1 mechatronics: メカトロニクス。mechanism（機械工学）と electronics（電子工学）を統合した概念であり、機械の制御などにコンピューターを導入し、高性能化・自動化・省力化を図るものである。
＊2 glocal business: グローカル経営。「グローカル」は global と local の合成語であり、地球規模でありながらも各地域に根ざした経営のあり方をいう。
＊3 Industrie4.0: 第4次産業革命。ドイツが推進する製造業の技術革新。
＊4 Internet of Things (IoT): モノのインターネット。インターネットに様々な機器や装置をつなげ、相互に情報伝達できるようになることを意味する
＊5 Vision 2025: 2025年ビジョン。安川電機が掲げる長期経営計画の名称。

Exercise 1

❖ Read the sentences below. Write T if the sentence is true, F if it is false.

1. (　　) Yaskawa Electric Corporation is the first in the world to propose the concept of 'mechatronics.'

2. (　　) With a number of international business hubs, Yaskawa conducts business in the same manner in different countries.

3. (　　) Automation and labor saving have led to rising expectations for Yaskawa's solutions provided with servos and robots.

4. (　　) Yaskawa launched the new concept 'i^3-mechatronics' in 2017, and its 'i^3' represents integrated, intelligent and innovative.

5. (　　) They call their next-generation production factory in Saitama 'YASKAWA Cockpit.'

株式会社安川電機

産業用ロボットは累積台数世界トップクラスの実績を持つ 1915 年（大正 4 年）設立の会社です。「事業の遂行を通じて広く社会の発展、人類の福祉に貢献する」という経営理念に基づき、“モータの安川” から “オートメーションの安川” を経て、“メカトロニクスの安川” へと事業の主体を変化させてきました。現在では、メカトロニクス製品にデータ活用を融合させ、顧客の持続的な生産性向上を実現するソリューションコンセプト「i^3-Mechatronics」でビジネスを更に進化させています。なお、i^3（アイキューブ）とは、“integrated (統合的)” “intelligent (知能的)” “innovative (革新的)” の「3 つの i」を意味しています。

本社は福岡県北九州市にありますが、独自制御技術でサーボモーターでは世界首位であり、また四半期決算で上場企業の初めに発表があるため、安川電機の決算状況は中国の景気や欧州の景気動向の先行指標とみられています。

Exercise 2

Listen to the sentences and fill in the blanks. 50

1. Since its (   ), Yaskawa Electric Corporation has been (   ) for a technology-(   ) company.
2. 'Motion (   )' is one of Yaskawa's (   ) technologies, along (   ) 'robotics' and 'power conversion.'
3. Yaskawa (   ) a 'glocal business,' which is (   ) by considering local conditions in (   ).
4. Circumstances (   ) manufacturing industries all (   ) the world are changing (   ).
5. With their new (   ) data solution, they can secure and (   ) high (   ).
6. Yaskawa's latest tool (   ) us to collect and (   ) data in a comprehensive (   ).
7. They (   ) a leading-edge (   ) in (   ), which utilizes IoT and AI.
8. The company will always make (   ) to (   ) the high expectations from their (   ).

Exercise 3

Listen and fill in the blanks in the short conversations below. Then practice the conversations with a partner. 51

1. *Student:* When was the word 'mechatronics' (   ) used?

   Company: We pioneered this (   ) in the late (   ) merging 'mechanism' and 'electronics,' and now it is (   ) used around the world.

2. *Student:* What were the main (   ) of Yaskawa (   ) the beginning?

   Company: We started with the production of (   ) for coal mines and have (   ) the development of our motor technology for more than (   ) years.

3. *Student:* How (   ) are servo motors from (   ) motors?

   Company: Not only (   ) continuously, they respond very (   ) and swiftly.

Exercise 4

❖ Rearrange the words and phrases to make correct sentences.

1. 株式会社安川電機は、1977 年に全電気式産業ロボットを発売して以来、世界の産業用ロボット市場をリードしている。
YASKAWA Electric Corporation has led the world's industrial robot market (1977, robot, release, industrial, first, all-electric, since, the, in, of, the).

2. 産業用ロボットは、形によってではなく、その機能にしたがって定義される。
Industrial robots (according, functions, shape, their, defined, but, are, not, to, by).

3. 私たちの会社は、製造活動に伴う負荷を減らすことで、環境に貢献している。
Our corporation (the environment, the burdens, contributes, reducing, result, that, by, to) from manufacturing activities.

Exercise 5

❖ Translate into English.

1. モーター（a motor）は、電気エネルギーを力学的エネルギー（mechanical energy）に変換する（convert）装置である。

2. 安川電機（Yaskawa Electric）の製品は、世界最高レベルの性能（performance）を誇る。

CHAPTER 14

ヤマト運輸株式会社

Yamato Transport Co., Ltd.

クロネコヤマトの宅急便

Pre-Reading 1 : Key Words

❖ Match each word with its definition below.

＊The words are listed in the order in which they appear in the reading.

1. found
2. launch
3. feedback
4. adapt
5. renovate
6. logistics
7. measure
8. optimization

(　　) a. to modernize; make new again

(　　) b. an action planned or taken to achieve a desired result

(　　) c. to begin

(　　) d. response; comments and remarks

(　　) e. the commercial activity of transporting goods to customers

(　　) f. to become familiar with a new situation

(　　) g. the process of making something as good or effective as possible

(　　) h. to establish

Message from the President

52

Yamato Transport Co., Ltd. was [Pre1]founded in 1919. After starting Japan's first delivery business based on fixed truck routes《トラック路線事業》 in 1929, we went on to [Pre2]launch our TA-Q-BIN business in 1976.

TA-Q-BIN was launched based on the idea of "Next-day delivery of parcels between personal customers." After TA-Q-BIN's launch, we have continued to bring out《世に出す》 a succession of new services including Golf TA-Q-BIN, Cool TA-Q-BIN, as well《and also》 as value-added services such as *1TA-Q-BIN Collect to contribute to the growth of the e-commerce《電子商取引》 market and the increasing number of *2Business-to-Customers" parcels. All of these were the result of [Pre3]feedback from customers.

The reason we could and will continue evolving while [Pre4]adapting to the changes in times is due to our unchanging commitment《取り組み》 to provide customers with services they will appreciate.

The Yamato Group celebrated its 100th anniversary in 2019. To further evolve in the next 100 years, we will continue to provide services to meet our customers' needs.

We do not simply deliver parcels. By adding both visible and invisible《有形無形の》 values to [Pre5]renovate our network, we aim to provide a brand new [Pre6]logistics network besides TA-Q-BIN. Also, we cooperate with local authorities to address《tackle; deal with》 problems such as low birth rates and the aging and declining population in Japanese rural communities as well as [Pre7]measures in case of natural disasters. At the same time, we are now also actively pursuing《進める》 new initiatives《構想、計画》 such as building a network of delivery lockers《宅配便ロッカー》 that can be used by any delivery company and joint driving operations《共同運行》 to achieve the [Pre8]optimization of the whole logistics industry, according to《～に応じて》 the changing times.

荷物受け渡し

To achieve that, we are currently making efforts in the promotion of working style reform to improve the working environment for our employees by the digitization of information and works. We will also speed up the development and use of new technologies including automatic driving and AI.

In order to further improve "TA-Q-BIN," we always consider how to change its system. We also think about how to please our customers with other solutions besides "TA-Q-BIN." To provide better services, we will sincerely listen to our customers' voices and think continuously.

We look forward to your continued support and encouragement as we pursue our goals.

出典 http://www.global-yamato.com/en/corporate/message.html

"TA-Q-BIN"— Our Delivery Service 53

宅急便車

Our TA-Q-BIN delivery service covers everything from parcel pickup to providing next-day delivery with just one phone call, 365 days a year. TA-Q-BIN comes from the Japanese words "taku" (home), "kyuu" (speedy), and "bin" (transport), and for Yamato, a company that takes customer convenience to the next level and provides a wide variety of services, our determination to deliver parcels even faster and more reliably is implied in the name.

出典 http://www.global-yamato.com/en/corporate/message.html

Kuroneko (Black Cat) — A Logo Known to Everyone in Japan 54

Yamato has locations throughout Japan. Our trucks and delivery staff provide services over the country every day, meaning that Yamato's Kuroneko logo can be seen in many places across Japan. The logo depicts a mother cat gently carrying a kitten in her mouth, which represents Yamato's approach to provide hospitable delivery services to all customers.

出典 http://www.global-yamato.com/en/about/

【Notes】

＊1 TA-Q-BIN Collect: 宅急便コレクト。商品代金を、代金引換・配達時クレジットカード払い・配達時電子マネー払いにより、荷物の受領時に決済を行うサービス。
＊2 "Business-to-Customers" parcels: 「法人からの」お荷物

Exercise 1

❖ Read the sentences below. Write T if the sentence is true, F if it is false.

1. (　　) It was in 1929 that Yamato Transport launched Japan's first"Route Freight Service"by truck.

2. (　　) Yamato's services such as Golf TA-Q-BIN and Cool TA-Q-BIN originated with its president.

3. (　　) Yamato's commitment to providing customers with appreciated services leads to its continued development.

4. (　　) As well as delivering parcels, Yamato aims to optimize the whole logistics industry.

5. (　　) Their top priority is to improve the working conditions for their employees.

ヤマト運輸株式会社

設立は 1919 年で、2019 年に創業 100 年を迎えました。クロネコヤマトの宅急便で有名な会社です。全国におよそ 4,000 拠点を擁し、宅配便国内シェア 44％で業界首位です。海外売上高比率は 2％ですが、アジア（中国・台湾・シンガポール・マレーシア・タイ）などに拠点があります。

2020 年 1 月に発表した中期的な経営のグランドデザインである「YAMATO NEXT100」に基づき、次の 100 年も第一線の社員がお客様にしっかりと向き合い「お客様の立場に立って考え、スピーディーにお応えできる」ヤマトであるために、組織再編やデジタルトランスフォーメーションによる物流オペレーションの効率化・標準化、データドリブン経営への転換、さまざまなステークホルダーとの共創によるオープンな物流インフラの構築、そしてサステナビリティの取り組みなど、グループの事業構造・基盤構造に対する抜本的な改革を進めています。

Exercise 2

❖ Listen to the sentences and fill in the blanks. 55

1. Yamato Transport is (   ) (   ) simply (   ) Kuroneko Yamato.
2. "TA-Q-BIN" is (   ) a (   ) (   ).
3. Yamato will (   ) evolving for the (   ) of all (   ).
4. Yamato (   ) its (   ) in Japan in (   ).
5. Delivery on the specified date and (   ) may not be possible (   ) to disasters, (   ) conditions, etc.
6. They (   ) (   )-(   ) logistics.
7. You see Kuroneko's delivery (   ) using a (   ) driven cart instead of a truck in (   ) or densely populated areas like Tokyo.
8. Yamato's logistics and distribution (   ) have become an important (   ) of social (   ).

Exercise 3

❖ Listen and fill in the blanks in the short conversations below. Then practice the conversations with a partner. 56

1. *Shuhei:* How (   ) do you use Yamato's delivery service?

   Etsuko: At least (   ) a month. Because my aunt is living in a nursing home, I have to (   ) some of her (   ) necessities.

2. *Student:* Your company (   ), a yellow oval with a black cat (   ) a kitten in her mouth, can be seen in many places. I wonder (   ) it symbolizes.

   Company: It represents our (   ) that items entrusted to us for (   ) will be treated with the utmost (   ).

3. *Keiko:* In my absence, I received an attempted delivery (   ) from Yamato Transport. So I have to (   ) redelivery online.

   Naoko: If I were you, I would use the (   ) phone service and specify the delivery (   ) period. It's very convenient for customers to be able to (   ) one from among (   ) time periods.

Exercise 4

❖ Rearrange the words and phrases to make correct sentences.

1. ヤマトグループは物流サービスの海外展開に積極的に取り組んで参ります。
   The Yamato Group (services, accelerate, of, logistics, will, overseas operations).

   ____

   ____

2. 「お客様に向き合う」をモットーに、私たちの会社はお客様のニーズをキャッチし、お客様に寄り添ったサービスをご提供し続けます。
   With the motto “all for the customers,” our company continues to understand (needs, customers’, services, provide, meet, them, that, and).

   ____

   ____

3. 日本の労働人口が減少する中、その会社はデータやAIやロボティクスなどの活用を推進してきている。
   As Japan’s working population shrinks, (promoting, firm, been, data, use, has, of, the, the), AI, robotics, and so forth.

   ____

   ____

Exercise 5

❖ Translate into English.

1. ヤマト運輸株式会社（Yamato Transport Co., Ltd.）は、1976年に日本で最初の個人顧客向けの (aimed at) 配送サービス（a delivery service）を開始した。

   ____

   ____

2. ヤマトグループ（the Yamato Group）は、約22万人の従業員を擁し、年間（annually）約18億個の荷物（parcel）を配送しています。

   ____

   ____

CHAPTER 15

株式会社リクルートホールディングス

Recruit Holdings Co., Ltd.

情報は社会を動かす

Pre-Reading 1 : Key Words

❖ Match each word with its definition below.

＊The words are listed in the order in which they appear in the reading.

1 . drastic
2 . alter
3 . benefit
4 . disparity
5 . mindset
6 . describe
7 . realization
8 . committed

(　　) a. attitude; a particular way of thinking

(　　) b. willing to work hard at something; dedicated

(　　) c. to receive an advantage

(　　) d. the act of achieving something that was planned or hoped for

(　　) e. a great difference

(　　) f. to change

(　　) g. to give an account of

(　　) h. radical; extreme

The goals of Recruit Group

57

Brand Logo

We are living amid rapid and [Pre1]drastic change. In the last three decades, we have seen computer processing speeds increase to the point that we now hold tremendously powerful [*1]smart devices in our pockets, paving the way for an ever-more《常に》 [*2]connected world and connected lifestyles.

Changes in the way that information and experiences are shared has transformed lifestyles, fundamentally [Pre2]altered economies, and had a colossal《enormous》 impact on society and the environment worldwide. Moreover, the frameworks and rules supporting this change have become burdensome《煩わしい》 and exceedingly complex. While many people take such progress for granted and enjoy the advantages of more freedom of choice when making life decisions《人生に関わる決断》, not everyone is [Pre3]benefiting from the shift《変化》. Rather, there is an increase in [Pre4]disparity between those who can leverage《活用する、活かす》 technology to process complex information and those who cannot. This gap also appears to have widened between countries, and even between different groups of people within countries.

Because of this, we believe that it is important that societies encourage《促す》 a [*3]"Follow Your Heart" [Pre5]mindset, where individuals can determine their own direction and create the lives that they wish to lead. Since our foundation, we have advocated for a brighter world where all individuals can live life to the fullest, and we truly believe that by offering increased opportunities to everyone, we can contribute to realizing such a world.

[*4]"Opportunities for Life. Faster, simpler and closer to you." represents Recruit Group's mission as inspired by the philosophy《企業理念》 [Pre6]described above. Based on this mission, we endeavor to meet the diverse needs of individual users and enterprise clients by providing the very best《最善の(=optimal)》 matching solutions through our ambition《念願、大望》 combined with our technology. It is my hope that, through [*5]this report, we can communicate to all of our stakeholders that our management philosophy is rooted in our daily activities.

[*6]The Sustainable Development Goals (SDGs[*1])—targets that the international community aims to achieve by 2030—declare first and foremost《真っ先に、何よりもまず》

株式会社リクルートホールディングス

the objective of realizing a society where all people can pursue larger freedom. Larger freedom means the opportunity to determine one's life through a multiplicity of choices, meaning that everyone can choose [*7]their own way of life. In this sense, Recruit Group's "Follow Your Heart" vision is perfectly aligned with《～と連携して[繋がって]》 the aim of humanity as a whole. We strongly believe that we can make a significant contribution to the [Pre7]realization of such a future, and we are [Pre8]committed to continuing to work towards these goals.

＊1 Acronym《頭字語》 of Sustainable Development Goals, which were adopted by the United Nations summit meeting in September 2015 and are goals for the 193 member countries to achieve in the 15 years from 2016 to 2030.

出典 https://recruit-holdings.com/who/message/

表彰制度

【Notes】

＊1 smart devices: スマートデバイス。スマートフォンやタブレット端末などの情報機器の総称。
＊2 connected: ネットワークを使える（環境にある）
＊3 "Follow Your Heart"：「自分の気持ちに素直に（生きる）」
＊4 "Opportunities for Life. Faster, simpler and closer to you."：「まだ、ここにない、出会い。より速く、シンプルに、もっと近くに」
＊5 this report: 統合報告書のこと。
＊6 The Sustainable Development Goals (SDGs*1): 持続可能な開発目標。2015 年の国連サミットで採択された "Sustainable Development Goals" の略称で、国連加盟 193 か国が 2016 年から 2030 年の 15 年間で達成するために掲げた目標。
＊7 their: この their は everyone を受けており、現代英語ではごく一般的な用法である。e.g. Everyone has good and bad moments in *their* life. That's what life's all about.

Exercise 1

❖ Read the sentences below. Write T if the sentence is true, F if it is false.

1. (　　) An ever-more connected world is followed by the emergence of smart devices.

2. (　　) There are some people out there who can't use technology effectively to deal with complex information.

3. (　　) They will create satisfaction that can only be achieved through the best matching of the information provided by their clients with the needs and requirements of individual users.

4. (　　) A massive amount of recruitment information makes it very easy for job seekers to choose the right kind of work.

5. (　　) Recruit Group's "Follow Your Heart" vision aims to realize a society where everyone can determine their own life through a large number of choices.

株式会社リクルートホールディングス

創業以来のノウハウを活用し、日常生活における分野でも情報を自由化し、個人が多様な選択肢から選べる世界の実現に貢献しています。最近ではメディア事業に限らず中小企業の業務支援にまで事業を拡大しています。また、会社全体としては、世界60か国以上で展開する求人情報検索エンジン「インディード」を主軸とした“HRテクノロジー”、国内における人材・販促分野のメディア事業を展開する“メディア＆ソリューション”、国内外で広く展開する“人材派遣”の3つの事業セグメントとなっています。

リクルートの歴史は、最適なマッチングにより世の中の「不」（社会の不満、不便、不安）の解消に寄与するビジネスの歴史とも言えます。今後も「一人ひとりが輝く豊かな世界の実現」に向け、同社は歩んでいくことでしょう。

Exercise 2

❖ Listen to the sentences and fill in the blanks.

1. We (　　　) to continue (　　　　　　) the best matching (　　　　　) available.
2. Since our (　　　　　　　), we have (　　　　　　　) individuals and businesses, offering both a (　　　　　　　) of choices.
3. We have developed our business to (　　　　) a world (　　　　　) people can (　　　　　) their hearts.
4. Looking (　　　　　), Recruit Group will aim to evolve its (　　　　　　) for better matching between users and (　　　　　　).
5. As (　　　　　) citizens, we strive to contribute to a (　　　　　　) society through all of our (　　　　　　) activities.
6. (　　　　　　) personally identifiable (　　　　　　　) and guarding (　　　　　　) information are their ongoing priorities.
7. Each one of us is (　　　　　　) to seeking out the (　　　　　) of society and taking (　　　　　) for a better future.
8. With "Indeed" you can (　　　　　) millions of (　　　　) online to find the next step in your (　　　　　).

Exercise 3

❖ Listen and fill in the blanks in the short conversations below. Then practice the conversations with a partner.

1. *Etsuko:* It seems I had my (　　　　　　　) stolen on the Net. I (　　　　) if it's because I often (　　　　) online shopping.

   Michiko: If you haven't taken (　　　　　　　) to protect your personal data, you need to improve (　　　　　　) and change your login (　　) and password.

2. *Naoko:* Why have (　　　　　　) apps grown in (　　　　　　) among job-seeking students?

   Shuhei: Because the tools (　　　) them meet (　　　　　　) alumni and more companies are using recruiters to find (　　　　　).

3. *Shunji:* What kind of (　　　) would you like to (　　　) if you change your (　　　　　)?

   Norihiko: I hope to (　　　) an IT-(　　　　　) job.

Exercise 4

❖ Rearrange the words and phrases to make correct sentences.

1. 1960年に創業した株式会社リクルートホールディングスは、現在では世界の潮流やニーズに合わせたサービスを提供しています。
   Founded in 1960, Recruit Holdings Co., Ltd. now (services, tailored, needs, offers, trends, global, and, to).

   ____

   ____

2. その会社は最適な選択肢を提供することに更に注力すべく取り組んでいる。
   They (proposing, focusing, working, optimal, choice, more, are, the, on, on).

   ____

   ____

3. ビジネスに関連するリスクを適切に管理し、対応することは重要です。
   It is important to (the business, the risks, appropriately, associated, manage, respond, with, and, to).

   ____

   ____

Exercise 5

❖ Translate into English.

1. リクルートホールディングス（Recruit Holdings）は、私たちの生活の多くの分野において幅広いサービスを提供している会社です。

   ____

   ____

2. 私たちは顧客のニーズを満たすことを優先しなければ（give priority to）ならない。

   ____

   ____

Leading the Way: Major Japanese Corporations [Second Edition]
日本を代表する企業で学ぶ 総合英語［改訂新版］ [B-927]

1刷 2021年2月16日
2刷 2023年3月31日

著　者 小 澤 健 志 Kenji Ozawa
小 泉 和 弘 Kazuhiro Koizumi
山 崎 千 秋 Chiaki Yamazaki
竹 内 裕見子 Yumiko Takeuchi
豊 岡 めぐみ Megumi Toyooka
早 坂 裕 介 Yusuke Hayasaka
山 下 理恵子 Rieko Yamashita

発行者 南雲一範 Kazunori Nagumo
発行所 株式会社 南雲堂
〒162-0801 東京都新宿区山吹町361
NAN'UN-DO Co., Ltd.
361 Yamabuki-cho, Shinjuku-ku, Tokyo 162-0801, Japan
振替口座：00160-0-46863
TEL: 03-3268-2311（営業部：学校関係）
03-3268-2384（営業部：書店関係）
03-3268-2387（編集部）
FAX: 03-3269-2486

編集者 加藤 敦
装　丁 Nスタジオ
組　版 Office haru
検　印 省 略
コード ISBN978-4-523-17927-6 C0082

Printed in Japan

E-mail nanundo@post.email.ne.jp
URL http://www.nanun-do.co.jp/